① 7-20-24

74

BAPTIZED WITH THE
HOLY
GHOST

A Pentecostal Perspective

GRANT RALSTON

AND

EDWARD RALSTON

WESTBOW
PRESS®
A DIVISION OF THOMAS NELSON
& ZONDERVAN

This book is a work of non-fiction. Unless otherwise noted, the author and the publisher make no explicit guarantees as to the accuracy of the information contained in this book and in some cases, names of people and places have been altered to protect their privacy.

WestBow Press books may be ordered through booksellers or by contacting:

WestBow Press
A Division of Thomas Nelson & Zondervan
1663 Liberty Drive
Bloomington, IN 47403
www.westbowpress.com
1 (866) 928-1240

Because of the dynamic nature of the Internet, any web addresses or links contained in this book may have changed since publication and may no longer be valid. The views expressed in this work are solely those of the author and do not necessarily reflect the views of the publisher, and the publisher hereby disclaims any responsibility for them.

Any people depicted in stock imagery provided by Getty Images are models, and such images are being used for illustrative purposes only. Certain stock imagery © Getty Images.

All Scripture quotations are taken from the King James Version.

ISBN: 978-1-9736-8655-2 (sc)
ISBN: 978-1-9736-8656-9 (hc)
ISBN: 978-1-9736-8654-5 (e)

Library of Congress Control Number: 2020903136

Print information available on the last page.

WestBow Press rev. date: 2/25/2020

CONTENTS

FOREWORD

I have pastored a Pentecostal church for nearly 25 years. I can't adequately articulate how excited I am for this work to be placed in the hands of our church. My father and oldest son have teamed up again to produce another powerful presentation of a vital aspect of Pentecostal theology. I have had the privilege of watching their lives very closely, and this work flows not only from personal study and formal training, but also from their respective experiences in the baptism of the Holy Ghost.

This week, I am in Brazil preaching on the subject "Evangelizing in the Power of the Holy Ghost." This title captures so well the words of Jesus in Acts 1:8 that prophesied his disciples would receive this blessed power to propel the church forward through persecution. This key aspect of the need for the Holy Ghost in the life of every believer is dealt with thoroughly as well as other important questions, such as "Do all believers speak in tongues when they are baptized in the Holy Ghost? Do you have to speak in tongues to be saved? Is speaking in tongues the only initial evidence of being baptized in the Holy Ghost? Are believers receiving the baptism of the Holy Ghost today?" These questions, along with many others, are dealt with fully and biblically in this book.

As you read *Baptized with the Holy Ghost: A Pentecostal Perspective,* I pray that a renewed desire for more of God's power is awakened in your soul. There is a need for each believer to receive the fullness of God's power! May it happen in your church like it did in Acts 2 and at the conference here in Brazil— "and they were all filled with the Holy Ghost" (Acts 2:4).

Ryan Ralston
President of Heritage Bible College

INTRODUCTION

There is a need for clear, sound, and <u>biblical</u> teaching concerning the Pentecostal view of the baptism of the Holy Ghost. Many Pentecostals have, perhaps subconsciously, "struggled to balance biblical teaching with their religious experience."[1] To be a Pentecostal is to believe in an experience of spiritual empowerment subsequent to conversion that is evidenced by speaking in tongues. This experience, taught clearly in the Scriptures, has been treated by some as the apex of spiritual maturity. In other words, according to them, once you speak in tongues, you have arrived spiritually, and there is little need for further instruction from the Bible.

This diminishing of the importance of doctrine is strange, considering that Pentecostals have always been committed to the authority of the Scriptures. Charles Conn, a well-known minister in the Church of God, wrote: "With the Pentecostal believer final authority for all spiritual inquiry rests in the Word of God. The Scriptures are the court of highest and final appeal."[2] Robert Menzies concurs, "Pentecostal faith and practice flow from the Bible... Pentecostals are 'people of the Book.' Although Pentecostals certainly encourage spiritual experience, they do so with a constant eye to Scripture."[3] Pentecostals have generally

---

[1] Stanley Horton, ed., *Systematic Theology: A Pentecostal Perspective* (Springfield, MO: Logion Press, 1994), 25.

[2] Wade Horton, ed., *The Glossolalia Phenomenon* (Cleveland, TN: Pathway Press, 1966), 24.

[3] Robert Menzies, *Pentecost: This Story Is Our Story* (Springfield, MO: Gospel Publishing House, 2013), 14.

maintained that the Bible is the ultimate authority for faith, life, practice, and doctrine. We should not believe something just because we have had extraordinary experiences; we should believe something because that is what the Bible teaches. Our experience can confirm what the word of God teaches, but it does not *determine* what it teaches. As Howard Ervin acknowledged, "Contemporary experience may (and does) illustrate, but only the biblical record adjudicates our conclusions. Whenever, therefore, contemporary witness to the Pentecostal experience is cited, it will be subordinated to the positive judgment of the Scriptures."[4]

On the other hand, in our effort to uphold the authority of the Scriptures, we should not ignore our spiritual experiences in the Holy Ghost. Many critics of the Pentecostal faith have asserted that Pentecostal theology is "based more on experience than on Scripture."[5] This may be partly true for certain individuals, as we have admitted previously. However, it is simply false to assert that *all* Pentecostals are Pentecostals only because they have been driven more by their experience in the Holy Ghost than by the Scriptures. We humbly submit our interpretations to the sacred text of Scripture and believe that speaking in tongues is the initial physical evidence of the baptism of the Holy Ghost, not because our experience dictates this conviction, but because our "Pentecostal experience and practice is *driven and shaped by the Bible*, particularly the narrative of Acts."[6]

As a matter of fact, we believe that the critics of Pentecostalism "do not really accept the full authority of Scripture."[7] As J. Rodman Williams observes: "When some of them come to passages dealing with the outpouring of the Holy Spirit and

---

[4] Howard M. Ervin, *Spirit-Baptism: A Biblical Investigation* (Peabody, MA: Hendrickson Publishers, 1987), 3.

[5] J. Rodman Williams, *Renewal Theology: Systematic Theology from a Charismatic Perspective*, Book 2 (Grand Rapids, MI: Zondervan, 1996), 242.

[6] Menzies, *Pentecost*, 9. Italics mine.

[7] Williams, *Renewal Theology*, 243.

the gifts of the Spirit, they subtly deny the force of what is said by relegating the passages to past history and in various other ways downplay their significance."[8] Instead of accepting the book of Acts as normative for church history, they argue that these passages were "unique" occurrences and were not intended to continue throughout the church age. Williams' conclusion is accurate: "By their *lack* of experience they settle for a limited view of the Bible's full authority and normativity."[9]

Rather than limiting the events in Acts in time to the first few years of the church, we Pentecostals believe that "the experiences described in Acts should serve as a model for contemporary Christian experience"[10] The aim of this book is to demonstrate convincingly why the Pentecostal perspective of the baptism of the Holy Ghost is correct. Through this effort, we seek to show that this precious experience is available to every child of God, what advantages this "promise of the Father" (Acts 1:4) offers to the Christian, and how each believer can receive it by faith.

Now, it must be admitted upfront that this book is not written by outsiders with no experience of Pentecost. Both authors have received the gift of the Holy Ghost with the evidence of speaking in tongues and have been engaged in ministry in Pentecostal churches. I (Edward) have been in Pentecostalism my entire life. In the late 1940s, my parents were saved and led into the Pentecostal blessing. My childhood was filled with dynamic manifestations of Pentecostal preaching and power. In 1962, I received Jesus Christ as my personal Lord and Savior, and two years later, I was baptized in the Holy Ghost. Later, I was called by God into the ministry, and after fifty years, I have witnessed miraculous healings, manifestations, and the gifts of the Holy Ghost in operation. Both my father and my son were miraculously

---

[8] Ibid.
[9] Ibid. Italics his.
[10] Menzies, *Pentecost*, 12.

healed by the power of God of serious illnesses. We desperately need the fullness of the Spirit and the demonstrations of the Holy Ghost in our midst during these tumultuous times.

I (Grant) am the grandson of Edward Ralston, born to his only son Ryan. Just like Grandpa, Dad also received salvation and the baptism of the Holy Ghost during his teenage years and was called into the ministry shortly thereafter. Soon after my birth, Dad assumed the pastorate of Savannah Holy Church of God, where he has continued his pastoral role to this day. Thus, for the entirety of my life, I have been raised in a Pentecostal preacher's home and encouraged to seek all that God has to offer in the twenty-first century, which includes speaking in tongues as the Spirit gives utterance (Acts 2:4). Such was *my* experience on June 26, 2011! After a few months of desperately seeking God, I was filled with the Holy Ghost and began to speak in tongues, with my Dad on one side of me and my Grandpa on the other side. I would be a foolish man to discount my experience in the Holy Ghost.

It would be impossible and illogical to deny or downplay our experiences with God. Thus, as you can see, we write as biased for the Pentecostal blessing of the baptism of the Holy Ghost. We are in a similar position as Roger Stronstad, who wrote an excellent book entitled *The Charismatic[11] Theology of St. Luke*. In the introduction to this wonderful defense of the Pentecostal perspective, he openly admits his spiritual encounters and explains why this influences his reading of Scripture:

---

[11] Don't be scared of Stronstad's use of the term "charismatic." He doesn't use the term to "describe the neo-pentecostal movement that penetrated the historical denominations of the 1960s and 1970s" (Roger Stronstad, *The Charismatic Theology of St. Luke* (Grand Rapids, MI: BakerAcademic, 2012), 16). Instead, he uses it to depict "God's gift of his Spirit to his servants, either individually or collectively, to anoint, empower, or inspire them for divine service" (ibid.)

I also write from within the tradition of Pentecostalism—that is, as one who has been baptized in the Holy Spirit with the attesting sign of speaking in other tongues. A believer who has spoken in tongues, been empowered by the Spirit, manifested the gifts of wisdom and knowledge, received visions, and so on, is not likely to interpret Luke's reports about the presence and activity of the Holy Spirit as simply words—sentences and paragraphs on a page to be analyzed and pushed and pulled in any and every direction.[12]

It must be emphasized, though, that bias does not mean error. No individual is perfectly neutral in his beliefs. He has been influenced by his experiences, his peers, and his family. Sadly, many people, for a variety of reasons, are biased *against* the Pentecostal perspective. We gladly acknowledge our experiences in the Holy Ghost. Still, we recognize that our experiences must be tested according to the Bible. Fortunately, the word of God confirms our experiences and challenges those who deny the validity of Pentecostal worship.

Before launching into the rest of the book, an issue of terminology needs to be addressed and explained. Throughout Acts, Luke employs various terms to describe the baptism of the Holy Ghost. The disciples were "filled with the Holy Ghost" (2:4). At Cornelius's house, "the gift of the Holy Ghost" was poured out (10:45). The Samaritan believers "received the Holy Ghost" (8:17) when Peter and John laid hands on them and prayed for them. John Wyckoff observes that "Pentecostals generally hold that such phrases are synonymous terms for the same experience of the Holy Spirit."[13] Indeed, in every case, "it is the Pentecostal

[12] Ibid., xiv.
[13] Horton, *Systematic Theology*, 426.

experience that is described," leading Howard Ervin to conclude that Luke "described the experience by a variety of synonymous expressions."[14] Because no single expression is sufficient to "adequately convey the full meaning of this event," by employing a variety of terms, Luke ensured that "distinctive and important nuances" to the baptism in the Holy Ghost would be underscored. Thus, in this book, we will also use these terms interchangeably, as Luke did, in our efforts to articulate and protect the Pentecostal experience.

We hope that this book is a blessing to you. Whether you are a Pentecostal with a desire to strengthen the reasons for your belief in tongues as the "initial evidence" or a non-Pentecostal inquiring about the convictions of your Pentecostal friend, may this book be a voice of clarity. May it be an invitation to receive all that God graciously offers to his children. May it be an inspiration to seek more of God. We pray that you will not only learn more about being baptized with the Holy Ghost but enjoy for yourself the truths that are contained within *Baptized with the Holy Ghost: A Pentecostal Perspective.*

---

[14] Ervin, *Spirit-Baptism*, 35.

CHAPTER 1

"Have Ye Received the Holy Ghost?" (Acts 19:2)

Many Christians have expressed their belief that the baptism with the Spirit is a subsequent work of God that follows receiving salvation. For example, R. A. Torrey, in his book *The Person and Work of the Holy Spirit*, wrote: "The baptism with the Holy Spirit is an operation of the Holy Spirit distinct from and additional to His regenerating work."[15] To defend this statement, he cites Acts 1:5, arguing that even though "the disciples had not as yet been baptized with the Holy Ghost... the men to whom Jesus spoke these words were already regenerate men."[16] Although we disagree with Torrey about what the biblical evidence is for the baptism of the Holy Ghost (he was not a Pentecostal), we applaud his ability to discern that "a man may be regenerated by the Holy Spirit and still not be baptized with the Holy Spirit."[17]

Likewise, Pentecostals hold to an experience that follows conversion. Thus, as L. Thomas Holdcroft notes, "The fact of the baptism in the Holy Spirit is not uniquely a Pentecostal belief; what is unique in Pentecostalism is that tongues are the evidence

---

[15] R. A. Torrey, *The Person and Work of the Holy Spirit* (Grand Rapids, MI: Zondervan, 1974), 174.

[16] Ibid.

[17] Ibid., 176.

1

of that baptism."[18] Pentecostals believe that being baptized in the Holy Ghost is always accompanied by speaking in tongues and that it serves the purpose of empowering the individual to be a more effective witness for Christ (Acts 1:8). We will examine the biblical account of this post-conversion experience in this chapter, since "before we can speak of evidence, we must first establish the validity of the experience which it purports to validate."[19] In the following chapters, we will describe what the biblical evidence of the baptism of the Holy Ghost is and why this experience is crucial toward fulfilling the Lord's command to make disciples of all nations.

That Pentecostals believe in an encounter with the Holy Spirit after salvation seems to be without controversy. Duffield and Van Cleave, Pentecostal preachers and teachers, observed: "The baptism with the Holy Spirit is subsequent to, and distinct from, His regenerative work... This distinction must be made, because many are genuinely saved who have never been filled with the Spirit."[20] Robert Menzies contends that one of "the three tenets" that has received "widespread acceptance" amongst Pentecostals is "that the baptism in the Holy Spirit (Acts 2:4) is a *post-conversion* enabling for mission."[21] Donald Johns concludes, "Being baptized in the Holy Spirit is something distinct from conversion. It can occur within the same time frame as conversion, but it is distinct.

---

[18] L. Thomas Holdcroft, *The Holy Spirit: A Pentecostal Interpretation* (Springfield, MO: Gospel Publishing House, 1979), 120.

[19] Robert Menzies in Gary B. McGee, ed., *Initial Evidence: Historical and Biblical Perspectives on the Pentecostal Doctrine of Spirit Baptism* (Eugene, OR: WIPF & STOCK, 1991), 221.

[20] Guy P. Duffield and Nathaniel M. Van Cleave, *Foundations of Pentecostal Theology* (Los Angeles, CA: Foursquare Media, 2008), 310.

[21] Menzies, *Pentecost*, 12. Italics mine. The other two unique elements of Pentecostal Theology, according to Menzies, is "that the experiences described in Acts should serve as a model for contemporary Christian experience" and "that speaking in tongues marks this experience."

Conversion involves the establishing of relationship with God; being baptized in the Spirit involves initiation into powerful, charismatic ministry."[22] Clearly, then, an essential aspect of Pentecostal theology is a belief in an experience that follows conversion.

The Pentecostal argument for a post-conversion experience depends primarily upon the book of Acts. In his wonderful defense of the Pentecostal position of being baptized in the Holy Ghost, Carl Brumback provided a reasonable explanation for why Acts ought to be used in the construction of this important doctrine. He wrote:

> When we know definitely what kind of baptism the New Testament believers received, we can be assured that THAT is the kind of baptism God desires to give us; we can compare our experiences with THAT, and rest content only when we have THAT. Now where in the Scriptures is the logical place to find THAT?.... If we are to discover what definitely took place when one was baptized or filled with the Spirit in the early church, we must turn to the Book of Acts, the experience book of the New Testament Church. There alone can we find a detailed description of the baptism or filling with the Spirit which was experienced by those early believers.[23]

Not everyone agrees with this approach. Brumback anticipated a common criticism of this method: "Some have raised the objection that doctrines should be based upon Biblical teachings,

---

[22] McGee, *Initial Evidence*, 162.

[23] Carl Brumback, *What Meaneth This? A Pentecostal Answer to a Pentecostal Question* (Springfield, MO: Gospel Publishing House, 1947), 184-185.

rather than upon Biblical experiences."[24] In other words, many who ridicule the Pentecostal position argue that we should base our doctrines on the "teaching" portions of Scripture, instead of the "narrative" passages. John Stott, author of *The Baptism and Fullness of the Holy Spirit*, expressed the belief that we should not build doctrine from the book of Acts: "This revelation of the purpose of God in Scripture should be sought in its *didactic*[25] rather than its *historical* parts. More precisely, we should look for it in the teachings of Jesus, and in the sermons and writings of the apostles, and not in the purely narrative portions of the Acts."[26] He concluded, "A doctrine of the Holy Spirit must not be constructed from descriptive passages in the Acts."[27]

To many students of the Bible, this seems to be inadequate and arbitrary. Should we not base our doctrines on the whole counsel of Scripture? This methodology is guilty of creating a false dilemma. Both the narrative and the teaching portions of the Bible should be viewed as able to teach doctrine. As a matter of fact, Paul himself refutes the theology of Stott: "All scripture is given by inspiration of God, and is profitable for *doctrine*..." (2 Timothy 3:16). When Paul penned these powerful words about the divine origin of the Scriptures, he had in mind the Old Testament, which includes historical material. The "unbiblical dichotomy between the so-called descriptive (historical, narrative) and didactic (teaching) passages of Scripture"[28] has resulted in many Christians reading the book of Acts as merely an interesting history of the early church void of much relevance for the contemporary church.

---

[24] Ibid., 186.

[25] Didactic is a fancy word that simply means teaching.

[26] John Stott, *The Baptism and Fullness of the Holy Spirit* (Downers Grove, IL: InterVarsity, 1964), 8.

[27] Ibid., 18.

[28] Stronstad, *The Charismatic Theology of St. Luke*, 7.

• Stanley Horton is correct: "The Bible does not give us history to satisfy our historical curiosity but rather to teach truth."[29]

Luke certainly had a *historical* interest in chronicling the spread of the gospel in the first century. His accuracy as a historian has been noted by a plethora of influential scholars.[30] However, his aim was not merely to record the bare facts of history. He strives "to teach and persuade."[31] Darrell Bock described the book of Acts as a "sociological, historical, and *theological* work…"[32] Thus, in the words of Roger Stronstad, "Since Luke has a theological interest, his narratives, though they are historical, are always more than simply descriptions or the record of brute facts."[33] To put it another way, though Luke exercised extreme caution as a *historian* of the awe-inspiring acts of God, he also wrote as a *theologian,* and we do ourselves a disservice when we only appreciate the reliability of his work but devalue his theological contribution.

This takes us back to 2 Timothy 3:16. If Paul considered the Old Testament historical narratives to be capable of teaching doctrine for Christians, then it would "be most surprising if Luke, who modeled his historiography[34] after Old Testament historiography, did not invest his own history of the origin and spread of Christianity with a didactic significance."[35] The insistence by some that "a doctrine of the Holy Spirit must not be constructed from descriptive passages in the Acts" contradicts what Paul wrote to Timothy. Instead of arbitrarily basing doctrine on only certain portions of Scripture, we should carefully consult the *entire* Bible and allow it to interpret itself. L. Thomas Holdcroft

---

[29] Stanley Horton, *Acts* (Springfield, MO: Logion Press, 2012), 18.

[30] Darrell L. Bock, *Acts.* Baker Exegetical Commentary on the New Testament (Grand Rapids, MI: Baker Academic, 2007), 9.

[31] Ibid., 11.

[32] Ibid., 2. Italics mine.

[33] Stronstad, *The Charismatic Theology of St. Luke*, 9.

[34] Historiography refers to the writing of history.

[35] Ibid., 8.

is exactly right: "The *whole* New Testament is relevant as the theological and experiential foundation for those who comprise the Christian Church."[36]

How does this relate to the Pentecostal doctrine of a post-conversion experience? As previously mentioned, the Pentecostal perspective relies heavily upon the book of Acts. Understanding that "Luke never intended to give his readers a simple description of events" helps us to see that "the historical accounts of the activity of the Spirit in Acts lay the groundwork for a doctrine of the Spirit that has normative implications for the mission and religious experience of the contemporary church."[37] Furthermore, Acts describes the coming of the Spirit, so it seems logical to study what Luke wrote in this magnificent history of the early church to ensure that our understanding of the Holy Ghost is accurate. J. Rodman Williams explained with clarity why the Pentecostals' dependence on the book of Acts for establishing their perspective on the baptism of the Holy Ghost is acceptable:

> A proper methodology entails, wherever possible, giving priority to the narrational and descriptive over the didactic. For example, in regard to the study of the Incarnation, it is better to begin with the narratives in the Gospels before proceeding to the briefer references and interpretation in the Epistles. This is likewise true about the coming of the Holy Spirit. Since Acts is the actual record of this event, its narration is the primary place to gain perspective and understanding.[38]

With some preliminary problems addressed, we are now able to proceed to look at the biblical evidence for the Pentecostal

---

[36] Holdcroft, *The Holy Spirit*, 110. Italics mine.

[37] Stronstad, *The Charismatic Theology of St. Luke*, 10.

[38] Williams, *Renewal Theology*, 182.

• position. It will be the goal of this chapter to demonstrate that people can be saved and born of God without having received the baptism of the Holy Ghost. Once we have established the existence of this post-conversion encounter, we will examine the biblical evidence for this experience in the next chapter.

A Case for a Separable Experience

Persecution was a frequent occurrence in the book of Acts. Those who rejected the gospel of Christ ferociously attacked these early disciples of Jesus. And they didn't persecute only the apostles, like Peter and John. On the contrary, every believer was subject to this vicious oppression. Stephen, "a man full of faith and of the Holy Ghost" (Acts 6:5), who "did great wonders and miracles among the people" (Acts 6:8) in the name of Christ and by the power of the Spirit, is known universally as the first Christian martyr. Stephen's martyrdom began what Luke described as "a great persecution against the church which was at Jerusalem" (Acts 8:1). However, as is often the case, the persecution did not stop the spread of the gospel. Rather, it actually forced the early disciples to be "scattered abroad" (Acts 8:2). What did these zealous, bold, committed followers of "this way" (Acts 9:2) do during their forced departure from Jerusalem? Luke informs us: "They that were scattered abroad went everywhere preaching the word" (Acts 8:4).

Included within this group of Christians was Philip, who "went down to the city of Samaria, and preached Christ unto them" (Acts 8:5). The people listened to what Philip preached and observed "the miracles which he did" (Acts 8:6). The demon-possessed were delivered from unclean spirits, and "many" who were afflicted with a variety of illnesses were healed (Acts 8:7). The result of these manifestations of God's power is overwhelming and widespread: "There was great joy in that city"

(Acts 8:8). Because the Samaritans believed what Philip preached "concerning the kingdom of God, and the name of Jesus Christ, they were baptized, both men and women" (Acts 8:12). Even Simon, the man who "used sorcery" to bewitch "the people of Samaria" and who was regarded as "the great power of God" (Acts 8:9,10), believed Philip's message and was baptized.

It is necessary to observe at this point that those who had believed the preaching of Philip and were baptized had been genuinely saved. Evidently, Philip had considered their profession of faith to be genuine, since he baptized them in water as a confirmation of their conversion. In the Bible, only believers are qualified to receive water baptism. For instance, on the Day of Pentecost, in response to Peter's sermon, "They that gladly received his word were baptized" (Acts 2:41). To put it differently, not everyone in the audience was baptized. However, anyone who heeded Peter's exhortation to "save [themselves] from this untoward generation" (Acts 2:40) was baptized. The Samaritan believers, including Simon, had "received the word of God" (Acts 8:14), which was confirmed by their being baptized. Darrell Bock contends that the phrase "received the word" is "yet another term for accepting the gospel."[39] Had their profession of faith been insincere or inadequate, Philip would not have baptized them in water.

That the Samaritans' belief was authentic is a fact recognized by a variety of commentators. F. F. Bruce observed, "The Samaritan *believers*, although baptized by Philip… had not at the same time received the gift of the Holy Spirit. But when Peter and John came to their city, they prayed for them, asking God to grant them the Holy Spirit, and then, when they laid their hands upon the *converts*, the Holy Spirit came upon them."[40] Here, Bruce

---

[39] Bock, *Acts*, 331.
[40] F. F. Bruce, *Commentary on the Book of the Acts* (Grand Rapids, MI: Wm. B. Eerdmans Publishing Company, 1973), 181. Italics mine.

called those who had received Philip's preaching "believers" and "converts," two terms that certainly are not apt descriptions of unsaved individuals. I. Howard Marshall concurred with Bruce's assessment: "There is no clear evidence that the people were merely superficial in their belief."[41] To assert that the Samaritans were not saved, despite the fact that Luke explicitly states they believed and were baptized, would be to distort the Scriptures to align with our own theology.

Now, once the apostles in Jerusalem heard that the Samaritans had accepted the preaching of the cross, they dispatched two apostles, Peter and John, to pray for them, "that they might receive the Holy Ghost" (Acts 8:15). As Luke writes, even though the Samaritan believers had been baptized in the name of the Lord Jesus, the Holy Spirit had not yet fallen on any of them (Acts 8:16). So, what did they do? Luke concludes, "Then laid they their hands on them, and they received the Holy Ghost" (Acts 8:17). Thus, their reception of the Holy Ghost was subsequent to their conversion and followed their initial decision to receive Christ by a number of days. As J. Rodman Williams wrote, "Samaria was about a two days' journey from Jerusalem. By the time word about the Samaritans' faith had reached Jerusalem, and Peter and John had traveled to Samaria for ministry, at least four days, possibly even a week, would have elapsed."[42] Nevertheless, regardless of how much time elapsed before the Samaritans received the Holy Ghost, the verdict of Howard Ervin is sound: "The analysis of the context justifies the conclusion that these Samaritan converts received the baptism in the Holy Spirit after their conversion."[43] That people can be saved, as the Samaritans were, without having received the Holy Ghost demonstrates that these are two separate experiences. John Wyckoff agreed, "The fact Luke shows that the

---

[41] I Howard Marshall, *Acts*. Tyndale New Testament Commentaries (Grand Rapids, MI: Wm. B. Eerdmans Publishing Company, 1989), 156.

[42] Williams, *Renewal Theology*, 275.

[43] Ervin, *Spirit-Baptism*, 74.

experience of the baptism in the Holy Spirit can be subsequent serves to underscore that *it is a separable and distinctive experience.*[44]

The story of the Samaritans isn't the only example in the book of Acts where "the gift of the Spirit is being received by those who for some time have been walking the way of faith."[45] Consider the conversion of the Apostle Paul and his subsequent filling with the Holy Spirit. Paul was a terrible enemy of the church. According to his own testimony, he persecuted the church of God "beyond measure" and sought to destroy it (Galatians 1:13). As Luke described it, "He made havoc of the church," going from house to house and arresting any follower of Christ (Acts 8:3). He was not satisfied to squash the church in Jerusalem only, but he received permission from the high priest to extend his "threatenings and slaughter against the disciples of the Lord" (Acts 9:1) into Damascus, so that "if he found any of this way, whether they were men or women, he might bring them bound unto Jerusalem" (Acts 9:2). Paul was such a wicked man that his radical transformation shocked everyone who was well-acquainted with his bold efforts to exterminate Christians from the face of the earth. Those who heard of his complete change glorified God, saying, "He which persecuted us in times past now preacheth the faith which once he destroyed" (Galatians 1:23).

This history-altering conversion occurred as Paul journeyed toward Damascus to fulfill his desire to arrest anyone who belonged to the way of Jesus Christ. Before Paul reached his destination, a bright, blinding light shined down from heaven, and a voice thundered a penetrating question to Paul: "Saul, Saul, why persecutest thou me?" (Acts 9:4). No doubt, Paul felt that he was doing God's will by trying to terminate the church of God, but his zealous actions contradicted the plan and purpose of God. Not only had he misjudged what it was to accomplish God's will,

---

[44] Horton, *Systematic Theology*, 432. Italics mine.
[45] Williams, *Renewal Theology*, 274.

but by persecuting the church, he had actually been persecuting the Lord Jesus Christ. In response to Paul's question about his identity, the Lord replied: "I am Jesus whom thou persecutest" (Acts 9:5). With the revelation of Jesus Christ, Paul began to tremble, astonished by this dramatic sequence of events, crying out, "Lord, what wilt thou have me to do?" (Acts 9:6). The Lord issued strict commands, to which Paul responded with eager obedience.

This fascinating account of Jesus Christ's personal revelation to Paul could easily lead us astray from our task. However, our goal in this chapter is to establish the fact that salvation and being filled with the Holy Ghost are two different experiences. It is necessary, then, to demonstrate that Paul had been converted prior to Ananias's commission by God to visit Paul so that he would "be filled with the Holy Ghost" (Acts 9:17). Two facts stand out in this narrative that confirm our suspicion that Paul had been born again before receiving the Holy Ghost. More than likely, as J. Rodman Williams wrote, "It was at the moment of the vision vouchsafed to Paul on the road to Damascus that he became a new man in Christ."[46]

One piece of evidence that Paul was converted on the road to Damascus, and thus before his being filled with the Spirit, is that he immediately obeyed the Lord's commands. He acknowledged the lordship of Christ not only by calling Jesus "Lord" (Acts 9:5,6), but also by going into the city of Damascus and awaiting further instructions. Jesus Christ simply told him to "arise, and go into the city, and it shall be told thee what thou must do" (Acts 9:6). Paul complied without hesitation. As he later revealed, "I was not disobedient unto the heavenly vision" (Acts 26:19).

Unregenerate, unsaved individuals do not follow God's will and obey Christ unquestionably. They dare to defy his commandments and commit daily treason against his sovereign

---

[46] Ibid., 188.

rule. They walk "according to the course of this world, according to the prince of the power of the air… fulfilling the desires of the flesh…" (Ephesians 2:2,3). However, anyone who experiences the glorious work of salvation immediately displays the reality of his conversion by doing what God wants him to do. Therefore, the willing obedience of Paul serves as an obvious indicator that he had been dramatically transformed by this revelation of Jesus Christ.

A second corroborating factor is how Ananias addressed Paul when he met him in the house where Paul was staying. Ananias, "a certain disciple at Damascus" (Acts 9:10), had received a message from the Lord through a vision that he needed to go find "one called Saul of Tarsus," who was staying in the house of Judas (Acts 9:11). Apparently, Paul's reputation had preceded him, for upon hearing the Lord's orders, Ananias expressed fear and anxiety, since he too had heard about "how much evil [Paul] had done to [the] saints at Jerusalem" and how Paul had "authority from the chief priests to bind all that call on thy name" (Acts 9:13,14). The Lord comforted Ananias's apprehension by informing him that God had a unique plan for Paul's life, a plan that consisted of suffering for the sake of the gospel and proclaiming the gospel "before the Gentiles, and kings, and the children of Israel" (Acts 9:15,16).

So, eventually, Ananias surrendered to the Lord's wishes and found Paul exactly where he was said to be. When Ananias approached Paul, he laid his hands on him and said, "Brother Saul" (Acts 9:17). To some people, his usage of this familial term does not carry any significance, either because of ignorance concerning this biblical concept or because too much usage of it has resulted in its being trivialized. Nevertheless, in spite of these possible issues, Stanley Horton's judgment is correct: "By this he recognized that Saul was now a believer."[47] By calling him "brother Saul," Ananias

---

[47] Horton, *Acts*, 184.

shows that his previous suspicion concerning Paul's conversion has now disappeared and that he "takes Saul to his heart as a brother in Christ."[48] We wholeheartedly agree with the conclusion of Howard Ervin:

> From the preceding context, it is clear that Ananias knew who Saul was and why he had come to Damascus—to persecute believers there. He would never, therefore, have entered Saul's presence and addressed him as "Brother Saul," unless he had been assured in advance that Saul was, in very truth, a "Brother" in Christ. Saul must, therefore, have become a Christian, in the fullest sense of the word, before Ananias came to him.[49]

An illustration might be helpful in grasping the significance of how Ananias addressed Paul. Imagine that you are serving Christ in a part of the world that is hostile to Christianity. Men who follow Jesus faithfully will likely die a martyr's death because of how intensely unbelievers hate the people of God. Suppose that one of the leaders of this persecution against Christians is dramatically converted to Christ. God sends you a dream, instructing you to visit his house and pray for him that he would be filled with the Holy Ghost. You yourself have heard about this man's wickedness. You initially hesitate to heed God's direction, but after a period of time, you accept God's will and go to his house. Now, let me ask you this question. How would you address him? Unless you were completely convinced of the validity of his conversion, would you call him a brother, signaling that he was now a part of the family of God? Of course not. Neither would

---

[48] A.T. Robertson, *Word Pictures in the New Testament — Vol. III* (New York, NY: Richard R. Smith, 1930), 121.

[49] Ervin, *Spirit-Baptism*, 76.

Ananias have. Paul had been changed by Christ, and this was confirmed when Ananias called him "brother Saul" (Acts 9:17).

This brings us to our point of discussion. Paul was saved, but he had not been baptized in the Holy Ghost. That is one of the reasons why Ananias was commissioned by the Lord to go see Paul and pray for him: that he would receive his sight and be filled with the Holy Ghost (Acts 9:17). Paul had been gloriously saved prior to being filled with the Holy Ghost, a fact confirmed by how Ananias addressed him ("brother Saul") and by Paul's obedience to the Lord's directions. However, even though he was a part of the family of God, he lacked the power of the Holy Ghost that would enable him to fulfill his God-appointed task. Once Ananias arrived at Judas's house and located Paul, he laid hands on him, and Paul received the gift of the Holy Ghost. The connection between Paul's reception of the Spirit and his boldness in the proclamation of the gospel is displayed immediately, as "*straightway* he preached Christ in the synagogues, that he is the Son of God" (Acts 9:20).

For our purposes, the narrative of Acts 9 teaches that a person can be saved without having received the Holy Ghost. If you concede that Paul was converted on the road to Damascus, as we have argued so far, then you must acknowledge that "three days" (Acts 9:9) separated his conversion and his baptism in the Spirit. Perhaps, you deny that the instance of Paul is normative, arguing that the reason why these examples seem to teach a separate experience subsequent to salvation is "due to the unique historical situation during the initial stages of the church."[50] But this approach is arbitrary and driven not by an objective study of the Scriptures but by an effort to conform the word of God to a specific theological position. As mentioned previously, the book of Acts *does* teach doctrine. It is necessary for us to consider the entire Bible in order to arrive at biblical truth, not just certain

---

[50] Horton, *Systematic Theology*, 429.

passages that we prefer. An unbiased reading would support the contention that "Luke intends to teach that a distinctive, separable baptism in the Holy Spirit experience is normative for Christian experience in all times."[51] Luke's endeavor to teach this distinct experience subsequent to salvation is highlighted in the story of Paul's dramatic change and empowering for ministry.

We will examine one final passage in our defense of the Pentecostal position of a post-conversion experience. Although we could examine the story of Acts 2 with the original disciples who were baptized in the Holy Ghost or Cornelius's house in Acts 10, we will look closely at Acts 19 and see how it relates to the present conversation. About twenty-five years after the initial descent of the Holy Spirit on the day of Pentecost,[52] Paul found himself in Ephesus, where he discovered "certain disciples" (Acts 19:1). Based on these disciples' response to Paul's questioning, some interpreters do not consider the twelve men (Acts 19:7) to have been "believers, given their lack of the Spirit."[53] This perspective, however, runs contrary to the plain teaching of Luke. As Stronstad contended, "They, who manifest the sign of being baptized in the Spirit (19:6), are first reported to be disciples and believers (19:1,2)."[54] F. F. Bruce agreed that "these men were Christians" and that Paul's question about whether they had received the Holy Ghost "suggests strongly that he regarded them as true believers in Christ."[55]

One piece of evidence that confirms that these disciples were true believers in Christ is how Luke describes them: "certain disciples" (Acts 19:1). According to Stanley Horton, "Everywhere else in the Book of Acts where Luke mentions disciples he always

---

[51] Ibid.

[52] Ervin, *Spirit-Baptism*, 79.

[53] Bock, *Acts*, 599.

[54] Stronstad, *The Charismatic Theology of St. Luke*, 79

[55] Bruce, *Commentary on the Book of the Acts*, 385.

means disciples of Jesus, believers in Jesus, followers of Jesus."[56] The lone exception to this is Acts 9:25, where "the disciples" refers to Paul's disciples. However, to be a follower of Paul is to be a follower of Christ. As Paul wrote elsewhere, "Be ye followers of me, even as I also am of Christ" (1 Corinthians 11:1). Thus, Horton's contention withstands scrutiny. All twenty-six times that Luke used the term "disciples" in the book of Acts referred to followers of Jesus. The disciples that Paul found at Ephesus were no different.

However, this does not negate the fact that there was "something lacking in their experience."[57] Darrell Bock concurs with this analysis, arguing that "their instruction is incomplete, not that Jesus is not a part of it at all."[58] In other words, they are similar to Apollos of Alexandria, who is described as "an eloquent man" and "mighty in the scriptures" (Acts 18:24). He "was instructed in the way of the Lord; and being fervent in the spirit, he spake and taught diligently the things of the Lord, knowing only the baptism of John" (Acts 18:25). So, Apollos, armed with his knowledge of the Scriptures, came to Ephesus and "began to speak boldly in the synagogue" (Acts 18:26). Aquila and Priscilla, two Christians converted under the ministry of Paul, heard his passionate teaching but recognized a deficiency in his understanding of the gospel. Thus, they took him aside and "expounded unto him the way of God more perfectly" (Acts 18:26). Something similar happened with the disciples in Acts 19. Even though they believed in Jesus and were following him, they lacked some knowledge about the work of the Spirit.

Upon meeting these disciples, Paul asks them a question: "Have ye received the Holy Ghost since ye believed?" (Acts 19:2). This direct question signifies that there "could be a separation

---

[56] Horton, *Acts*, 316.

[57] Ibid.

[58] Bock, *Acts*, 599.

between saving faith and the experience of receiving the Holy Spirit."[59] Ralph Riggs's point is worthy of careful consideration:
• "If all disciples receive this experience of the Holy Spirit when they believe, why did Paul ask these disciples if they had done so? His very question implies that it is possible to believe without receiving the fullness of the Holy Spirit."[60] If so, this verse strengthens the Pentecostal position of [an experience subsequent to salvation.] Often times, this distinction can be obscured by the way the verse is translated. Stanley Horton succinctly defends the King James Version translation, explaining the reasoning behind it:

> Modern versions generally translate "since ye believed" (v. 2, KJV) as "*when* ye believed." But this translation is based on their theological presuppositions. The Greek is literally, "Having believed, did you receive?" "Having believed" (*pisteusantes*) is a Greek aorist (past) participle. "Did you receive" (*elabete*) is the main verb, also in the aorist. But the fact that they are both in the aorist is not significant here. The fact that the participle "having believed" is in the past is what is important, for the tense of the participle normally shows its relation to the main verb. Because this participle is in the past, this normally means that its action precedes the action of the main verb. That is why the King James translators, as good Greek scholars, translated the participle "since ye believed." They wanted to bring out that the believing must take place before the receiving.[61]

---

[59] Horton, *Acts*, 316.
[60] Ralph M. Riggs, *The Spirit Himself* (Springfield, MO: Gospel Publishing House, 1968), 54.
[61] Horton, *Acts*, 316-317.

Thus, it is possible to believe in Jesus without having received the Holy Ghost. J. Rodman Williams asserted, "There is the obvious implication that one believing may not yet have received the Holy Spirit. Initial faith is not necessarily accompanied by the gift of the Spirit."[62] Paul's very question implies that it is not a guarantee that those who have believed in Jesus Christ and his finished work will receive the Holy Ghost. Certainly, as Stronstad maintained, "Those who receive the Spirit in Luke-Acts are always first shown to have been those who are in right standing before God—that is, in every sense of the word, Christians."[63] Just because an individual is a Christian does not necessarily mean that he has been baptized in the Holy Ghost. These two experiences are distinguishable, as is implied by Paul's question to the disciples in Acts 19.

The disciples' response indicates that they were ignorant concerning the recent activity of the Holy Spirit: "We have not so much as heard whether there be any Holy Ghost" (Acts 19:2). Bock provides the meaning of this ignorance: "This probably does not mean that the disciples of John do not know that the Spirit exists... Rather, it means that they have not heard that the Spirit of God has come."[64] These disciples obviously know that the Holy Spirit existed. However, they did not know of his recent outpouring on the day of Pentecost. As Stanley Horton described it, "These disciples were really saying they had not heard about Pentecost or the availability of the baptism in the Holy Spirit."[65] After learning that they had only been baptized with John's baptism, Paul immediately proceeds to give them the fuller revelation: "John verily baptized with the baptism of repentance, saying unto the people, that they should believe on him which should come after him, that is, on Christ Jesus" (Acts

---

[62] Williams, *Renewal Theology*, 276.

[63] Stronstad, *The Charismatic Theology of St. Luke*, 79.

[64] Bock, *Acts*, 599.

[65] Horton, *Acts*, 318.

19:4). They received it gladly, demonstrating their commitment to Christ by submitting to water baptism "in the name of the Lord Jesus" (Acts 19:5).

This is the important part for our current discussion. Even though these men were followers of the way of the Lord, even though they had been baptized in water for the forgiveness of their sins (Acts 2:38), they had not yet received the Holy Ghost. The Holy Ghost did not fall on them until Paul had laid his hands on them (Acts 19:6). Obviously, there is a temporal distinction between their initial act of faith and their receiving the gift of the Holy Ghost. They were saved before they received the Spirit. J. Rodman Williams concludes, "The giving or receiving of the Holy Spirit is set against the background of salvation... Believing, again, precedes receiving... The coming of the Spirit presupposes the occurrence of salvation."[66]

Conclusion

Each of these accounts supports Stronstad's verdict: "In Acts the Spirit is given to those who are already Christians."[67] One additional observation confirms that the gift of the Holy Ghost was received by those who already were in a right relationship with God. Stronstad argues for what he calls "Luke's 'antecedent spiritual state' narrative strategy."[68] What exactly does this mean? He explains, "Luke always identifies the antecedent spiritual state of the person(s) he is about to report will receive the gift of the Holy Spirit."[69] For instance, before the Samaritans received the Holy Ghost, they are said to have believed the message of Philip and were baptized (Acts 8:12). Also, prior to the Holy Ghost's

---

[66] Williams, *Renewal Theology*, 190.
[67] Stronstad, *The Charismatic Theology of St. Luke*, 73.
[68] Ibid., 64.
[69] Ibid.

descent on the Ephesian believers, Luke makes note that they were disciples (Acts 19:1).

This becomes even more explicit given the fact that, as James Hamilton points out, "Luke records at least fifteen conversion accounts in Acts, and not one of these is described as a baptism in the Spirit."[70] When Sergius Paulus believed the word of God because he saw the miraculous judgment of the Lord against Elymas the sorcerer (Acts 13:12), Luke does not identify this conversion as a reception of the gift of the Holy Ghost. Similarly, after many people believed in the Lord because Peter, through the power of the Holy Ghost, raised Tabitha from the dead (Acts 9:42), he fails to mention that they were baptized in the Holy Ghost. Now, this is not to insinuate that these converts did not receive the Holy Ghost soon after they were saved. However, it is to suggest that Luke plainly distinguishes these two experiences. Thus, to assert that receiving the Holy Ghost occurs at the time of our initial faith would be to twist the scriptural account contained in the books of Acts and make it say what you want it to say.

In this chapter, we have defended the argument that the baptism of the Holy Ghost is a post-conversion experience. In other words, receiving the Holy Ghost is not the same thing as getting saved. We must be saved in order to receive the precious gift of the Holy Ghost. Now, what is the evidence that a person has received the Holy Ghost? According to the book of Acts, there was visible evidence that signaled that an individual had been baptized in the Holy Spirit. When someone received the Holy Ghost, he, along with those present, knew it immediately. In the next chapter, we will examine the evidence for the baptism of the Holy Ghost.

---

[70] Qtd in ibid.

CHAPTER 2

The Evidence of the Baptism of the Holy Ghost

L et's suppose that you are a new convert. Because of your passionate desire to learn more about God and his word, you lock yourself in a room for several months to pray and study the Bible diligently. Before your conversion, you literally had no knowledge of Christianity. Thus, you have not been biased in any direction, theologically speaking. Also, during your time of isolation, you *only* read the Bible and are thus not influenced by the opinions of prejudiced commentators, who are more interested in promoting a particular strain of theology than in explaining what the Scriptures truly teach.

After your separation from humanity, during which you grew "in grace, and in the knowledge of our Lord and Saviour Jesus Christ" (2 Peter 3:18), we ask you a simple question, "Do you believe that speaking in tongues is for today?" It is our firm conviction that you would undoubtedly respond in an affirmative manner. Indeed, an honest and objective reading of the New Testament would lead someone to expect that speaking in tongues is an available phenomenon. The Bible is crystal clear, in spite of the efforts of certain individuals to limit tongues to a bygone generation.

Jesus himself told his disciples that one of the signs that would follow "them that believe" was that "they shall speak with new tongues" (Mark 16:17). What is interesting is that this promise of tongues as an accompanying sign of believers follows on the heels of another promise: "He that believeth and is baptized shall be saved; but he that believeth not shall be damned" (Mark 16:16). Now, all Christians accept the continuance of the blessed promise that whoever receives the gospel will be saved. However, many deny the existence of tongues as a sign of believers. In his book *Ministry of Healing*, A. J. Gordon made this point powerfully:

> Both the one and the other ('he that believeth and is baptized shall be saved' and 'these signs shall follow them that believe') apply to ourselves down to the present day and indeed for all future time. Everyone applies the first part of the saying to ourselves, teaching everywhere that faith and baptism are necessary in all ages to salvation,[71] and that unbelief in all ages excludes from it. But what right has any to separate the words that Jesus immediately added from His former words! *Where is it said* that these former words have reference to all men and all Christians, but that the promised signs which should follow those who believe referred solely to the Christian of the first age? What God hath joined together, let not man put asunder.[72]

---

[71] We caution our readers against the false doctrine of baptismal regeneration, that is, water baptism is necessary for salvation. We do *not* believe that Gordon is espousing that perspective. Water baptism is an act of obedience to God's commandments. Any "believer" who refuses to be immersed in water has given ample reason to question the trustworthiness of his profession of faith. We receive water baptism not in order to be saved but because we are saved and are now publicly identifying with Christ. It is an external expression of an internal transformation.

[72] Qtd in Brumback, *What Meaneth This?*, 68-69.

Gordon's position exposes the lack of objectivity on the part of those who argue that speaking in tongues have ceased. To arbitrarily restrict the importance of "these signs" is to inflict damage on God's people by hindering their experience of all that he has for them. The burden of proof must surely lie on the shoulders of those who doubt the modern application of Paul's stern admonition: "Forbid not to speak with tongues" (1 Corinthians 14:39). By contending that speaking in tongues ceased early on in the history of the church, many are guilty of quenching the Spirit (1 Thessalonians 5:19) and stand in direct opposition to the teaching of God's word.

The point of this chapter is more than just to prove that speaking in tongues is a present reality, although such an endeavor deserves a lengthy treatment. We will attempt to demonstrate why speaking in tongues is *the* initial, physical evidence that a believer has received the baptism of the Holy Ghost. The aim of this book is to provide a biblical defense of the Pentecostal position on the baptism of the Holy Ghost, and this chapter will be dedicated to a crucial piece of that perspective.

Some may wonder why Pentecostals are so dogmatic about this insistence on speaking with tongues. Besides the fact that we consider this to be the clear teaching of Scripture, we honestly do not want Christians to attempt to live the Christian life without having received the gift of the Holy Ghost (Acts 2:38; 10:45). Carl Brumback speaks for us when he responded to those who accuse Pentecostals of creating "strife, division, and unrest in the Body of Christ" by spreading "such a controversial doctrine":

> In our insistence upon tongues, we are not contending for a pet doctrine, nor even for the glossolalia itself (blessed though it is!), but for that wonderful experience of which speaking with tongues is the initial, physical evidence. It is our sincere belief that without this evidence there

23

can be no fully Scriptural baptism with the Holy Ghost. Thus, to us, the value of speaking with tongues is, in one sense, commensurate with that of the baptism itself; though in another sense, it is of but relative importance, being simply a marvelous evidence of a marvelous experience.[73]

Before diving into the book of Acts and observing the biblical evidence of the baptism of the Holy Ghost, it is necessary to cite a few other Pentecostal authors to verify that this has been the traditional Pentecostal understanding. P. C. Nelson articulated the official Assemblies of God's position on the matter, "The Baptism of believers in the Holy Ghost is witnessed by the initial physical sign of speaking with other tongues as the Spirit of God gives them utterance (Acts 2:4)."[74] Brumback, again, provided an adequate summary of the Pentecostal perspective: "It is of a transcendent and miraculous character, producing extraordinary effects which are visible to the onlooker, *its initial oncoming being signalized by an utterance in other tongues*... In apostolic days speaking with tongues was a constant accompaniment of the baptism with the Holy Ghost, and should be in these days as well."[75] There should be unanimity amongst Pentecostals in relation to the question of whether speaking in tongues is the *initial* evidence of Spirit-baptism. To be a Pentecostal is to believe in a "baptism in the Spirit (Acts 2:4), understood as an empowering for mission, distinct from regeneration, *that is marked by speaking in tongues*."[76]

Now, just because Pentecostals insist that speaking in tongues is, unquestionably, the initial indicator that an individual has

---

[73] Ibid., 188.

[74] P. C. Nelson, *Bible Doctrines* (Springfield, MO: Gospel Publishing House, 1971), 85.

[75] Brumback, *What Meaneth This?*, 184,187. Italics mine.

[76] Menzies, *Pentecost*, 13. Italics mine.

received the Holy Ghost does *not* mean that we deny that there are additional signs that will accompany being filled with the Holy Ghost. In this chapter, we will focus, first and foremost, on the issue of what the *initial* evidence of being baptized in the Holy Ghost is, but we will also look at the *incessant* evidence. Lewis Willis summarizes the basic contention of this chapter:

> In accordance with the Scriptures, Pentecostals believe that those who are baptized in the Holy Spirit speak with other tongues. Again, in keeping with the scriptural record, Pentecostals believe that the speaking with tongues is the initial, empirical evidence of the Baptism in the Holy Ghost. They do not believe that speaking in tongues is the only evidence... They simply believe that glossolalia is the first overt and audible evidence that one has been baptized in the Holy Spirit[77]

The Initial Evidence

In the previous chapter, we began our discussion of the evidence for a post-conversion experience in Acts 8. We will again begin our examination here. If you recall, Peter and John laid their hands on the freshly converted disciples of Samaria, and they received the Holy Ghost (Acts 8:17). Pertinent to this chapter is the fact that Simon, the former sorcerer, perceived *something* that signified that "the Holy Ghost was given" (Acts 8:18). His eyes beheld something that indicated that the Holy Ghost had been received by the Samaritan believers. Howard Ervin asked the question that every student of the Bible must answer: "What did Simon see that convinced him that these Samaritan disciples

---

[77] Horton, *The Glossolalia Phenomenon*, 252.

had received the Holy Spirit through the laying on of the hands of Peter and John?"[78]

Some people will immediately point out that the passage does not directly state that they spoke in tongues. This is undoubtedly true. However, the fact that tongues are not mentioned does not *necessarily* imply that they did not speak in tongues. As Pentecostal preacher Joe Campbell asserted about this passage, "You say, the Bible does not say that they spoke in tongues. I answer you, 'Neither does it say that they did not speak in tongues.'"[79] Indeed, as we shall see, Luke mentions tongues three times in connection with the reception of the Holy Ghost (Acts 2:4; 10:46; 19:6). Since Luke records elsewhere that those who received the Holy Ghost spoke in tongues, it is acceptable to infer that the Samaritans also spoke with tongues when they were baptized in the Holy Ghost. Brumback's reasoning is correct: "It was not necessary for [Luke] to write of its presence in every instance of the baptism with the Spirit before we could accept it as the initial, physical evidence of that experience."[80]

The absurdity of this can further be exposed by considering a similar situation. In Acts 3, Peter and John go to the temple at the hour of prayer (Acts 3:1). On the way to pray, they meet a man who has been lame "from his mother's womb" (Acts 3:2). This encounter led to the lame man being healed in the name of Jesus. What was his reaction? Luke writes, "He leaping up stood, and walked, and entered with them into the temple, walking, and leaping, and praising God" (Acts 3:8). Now, this isn't the only time in the book of Acts where the lame are healed. Elsewhere, Luke notes, "Many… that were lame were healed" (Acts 8:7). This straightforward statement does not contain the same joyful

---

[78] Ervin, *Spirit-Baptism*, 73.

[79] Joe Campbell, *Warning! An Expose of the Devil's Counterfeit Offer Attempting to Popularize Pentecost* (Raleigh, NC: World Outlook Publications, n.d.), 73.

[80] Brumback, *What Meaneth This?*, 232.

reaction of the lame man in Acts 3. However, does this mean that there was no joyful reaction? Are we to infer that, because Luke fails to mention the reaction of the lame healed in Acts 8, there was no reaction? Of course not. The unreasonableness of this inference is self-evident. It is similarly absurd to claim that the Samaritans did not speak in tongues simply because Luke does not record their speaking in tongues.

So, what exactly did Simon see that informed him of the Samaritan's reception of the Holy Ghost? While the text does not exactly answer this question, and we must always guard against the temptation to go too far beyond what the Bible says, some reasonable answers can be supplied to satisfy our thirst for the truth. Amazingly, even commentators who are *not* Pentecostals accept that what Simon witnessed was, very likely, the Samaritan converts speaking in tongues. And, as Ervin noted, "There is considerable value in the answers given to this question by exegetes who cannot be accused of a Pentecostal bias."[81]

The great scholar A. T. Robertson, who taught at the Southern Baptist Theological Seminary, observed that the expression "when Simon saw" (Acts 8:18) demonstrates "plainly that those who received the gift of the Holy Spirit spoke with tongues."[82] Richard Lenski, a Lutheran commentator, concurred with Robertson: "The apostles laid hands on some of them, and these began to speak with tongues. *It was this that Simon saw* and that made him desire to possess the same ability he thought the apostles had."[83] F. F. Bruce's judgment is more reserved, but even his comments are supportive of the notion that the Samaritans spoke with tongues: "The context leaves us in no doubt that *their reception of the Spirit was attended by external manifestations* such as had marked His descent on the earliest disciples at

---

[81] Ervin, *Spirit-Baptism*, 73.

[82] Robertson, *Word Pictures*, 107.

[83] R. C. H. Lenski, *Commentary on the New Testament – Acts of the Apostles* (Peabody, MA: Hendrickson Publishers, 2001), 327. Italics mine.

Pentecost."[84] Finally, distinguished professor Darrell Bock of Dallas Theological Seminary wrote, "Although this text is not explicit, *an experience like Acts 2 and 10 is likely*... It obviously is something visible because Simon reacts when he sees its effect."[85]

We choose to side with these prominent, biblical scholars. When Peter and John laid their hands on the Samaritan believers, Simon was able to detect that, indeed, the Holy Ghost had been both given and received. What evidence convinced him of this? We are persuaded that, in the words of Bock, "an experience like Acts 2 and 10 is likely," namely, they spoke with tongues as the Spirit gave them utterance (Acts 2:4; 10:46). Once Simon saw the converts of Samaria speaking in tongues, he knew that the Holy Ghost had been given through the hands of the apostles.

Another example of tongues as the confirming sign that the Holy Ghost has been received is found in Acts 10. The story of how Peter wound up in Cornelius's house is staggering, but a full explanation of these providential events is beyond the scope of the present work. Suffice it to say, God brought it to pass that Peter would deliver the gospel to Cornelius, a God-fearing man (Acts 10:2), and his household. Peter began his sermon by noting that God is not a respecter of persons but accepts anyone in any nation who fears him and does what is right (Acts 10:34,35). He proceeded to describe the basic facts of the life, death, and resurrection of Jesus Christ. He instructed them that "remission of sins" is available for "whosoever believeth in [Jesus]" (Acts 10:43).

Peter's gospel presentation was divinely interrupted, however. Luke records that "while Peter yet spake these words, the Holy Ghost fell on all them which heard the word" (Acts 10:44). Later, in recounting this marvelous event, Peter added that this interruption occurred as he "began to speak" (Acts 11:15). Clearly, then, Cornelius and his house had accepted the further

---

[84] Bruce, *Commentary on the Book of the Acts*, 181. Italics mine.
[85] Bock, *Acts*, 332. Italics mine.

revelation of Christ contained in Peter's sermon, but they also received the gift of the Holy Spirit. The circumcised believers who had traveled with Peter stood in amazement, "because that on the Gentiles also was poured out the gift of the Holy Ghost" (Acts 10:45). Peter himself recognized this truth, evidenced by his insightful question: "Can any man forbid water, that they should not be baptized, which have received the Holy Ghost as well as we?" (Acts 10:47). Since the Gentiles had been baptized in the Holy Ghost, it would be absurd to deny them the privilege of water baptism in identification with Christ and his church.

We must emphasize the fact that Cornelius and his household did not experience a watered-down version when they received the Holy Ghost. Several statements from the book of Acts refute this assertion. In his summary to the church in Judaea who "heard that the Gentiles had also received the word of God" (Acts 11:1), Peter declares that "God gave them *the like gift* as he did unto us" (Acts 11:17). Furthermore, Peter observes that "the Holy Ghost fell on them, as on us at the beginning" (Acts 11:15). There is *every* indication in the passage that the Gentiles experienced exactly what those early believers experienced in the upper room (Acts 2). J. Rodman Williams concludes, "There is no suggestion that the coming of the Spirit in Jerusalem was a once-for-all matter, or that somehow what happened in Caesarea was secondary or subordinate."[86] Indeed, the congregation at Cornelius's house had received the Holy Ghost just like Peter and the rest had (Acts 10:47).

The question we must ask ourselves, though, is this: How did the circumcised believers know that the gift of the Holy Ghost had been poured out on the Gentiles? Luke writes, "*For they heard them speak with tongues, and magnify God*" (Acts 10:46). Because Cornelius and his household spoke in tongues, "the Jewish believers who accompanied Peter knew these Gentile

---

[86] Williams, *Renewal Theology*, 192.

converts had received the gift of the Holy Spirit."[87] William MacDonald agreed that it was the "glossolalia which made Peter and his six colleagues know with certainty that the Gentiles had received identically the same experience that he and the others had at the Pentecost feast."[88] J. Rodman Williams, again, observes, "Speaking in tongues was unmistakable evidence to Peter and those with him that the Caesareans had received the gift of the Holy Spirit."[89] The Gentiles had received the Holy Ghost, proven by the fact that they began to speak in tongues and glorify God.

Later in the book of Acts, another example occurs where those who receive the Holy Ghost speak in tongues (Acts 19:6). We examined this passage in the previous chapter, but it is relevant to the present discussion. As previously mentioned, when Paul found "certain disciples" (Acts 19:1) in Ephesus, he asked them a question, "Have ye received the Holy Ghost since ye believed?" (Acts 19:2). Earlier, we focused on how this inquiry (and the ensuing conversation between Paul and these disciples) supports the Pentecostal position of a post-conversion work of the Holy Spirit, but we must consider it again as it relates to the biblical evidence for the baptism of the Holy Ghost.

Upon thoughtful reflection, Paul's question hints that they could know for certain whether they had received the Holy Ghost. P. C. Nelson employs this argument:

> His question implied that... the reception of the Holy Spirit was so wonderful and was accompanied with such evidence that the recipients were able to answer the questions definitely... Suppose somebody had come along shortly after this and

---

[87] Ervin, *Spirit-Baptism*, 78-79.

[88] William G. MacDonald, "Glossolalia in the New Testament," *JETS* 7 (1964): 62.

[89] Williams, *Renewal Theology*, 212.

asked these twelve men the same question, do you suppose they would have been confused and unable to answer it?[90]

The answer to Nelson's question is that, of course, these twelve disciples at Ephesus would be able to answer confidently whether they had received the Holy Ghost. The reason why they could easily know if they had been filled with the Holy Ghost is that God chose a supernatural evidence to be the sign that would indicate that the gift had been given and received. When an individual receives the gift of the Spirit, he is immediately assured of his reception. As Duffield and Cleave ask, "If there were no particular supernatural evidence of the baptism with the Spirit by which it could be distinguished from all other operations of the Spirit, how could anyone be assured of the experience?"[91] God certainly was "not obligated to consult the opinion of man in making His sovereign choice of speaking with tongues"[92] to be the initial, physical evidence of being baptized with the Holy Ghost. However, we deem his decision to be wise, considering that "the recipient [of the Holy Ghost] will have no doubt whatsoever that he has indeed received the promise of the Father."[93]

To return to Acts 19, after Paul baptized them "in the name of the Lord Jesus" (Acts 19:5), he laid his hands on them, and "the Holy Ghost came on them" (Acts 19:6). As a result, the Ephesian disciples "spake with tongues, and prophesied" (Acts 19:6). F. F. Bruce comments about this passage, "When Paul had laid his hands on them, they received the Holy Spirit *in Pentecostal fashion*."[94] A. T. Robertson's observation is worth considering: "The speaking with tongues and prophesying was

---

[90] Nelson, *Bible Doctrines*, 89.

[91] Duffield and Cleave, *Foundations of Pentecostal Theology*, 324.

[92] Brumback, *What Meaneth This?*, 235.

[93] Duffield and Cleave, *Foundations of Pentecostal Theology*, 324.

[94] Bruce, *Commentary on the Book of the Acts*, 386. Italics mine.

external and indubitable proof that the Holy Spirit had come on these twelve uninformed disciples now fully won to the service of Jesus as Messiah."[95] Just like at Samaria and Caesarea, when the Holy Ghost fell on believers in Ephesus, those who received the Holy Ghost spoke in tongues. Importantly, speaking in tongues is mentioned *before* prophecy, further strengthening the case that it is the *initial* (not the only) evidence that the Holy Ghost has been received by a believer.

A discussion of the initial, physical evidence of the baptism of the Holy Ghost is incomplete, however, without briefly considering the first outpouring of the Spirit in Acts 2. Luke describes this first outpouring of the Holy Ghost beautifully:

> And when the day of Pentecost was fully come, they were all with one accord in one place. And suddenly there came a sound from heaven as of a rushing mighty wind, and it filled all the house where they were sitting. And there appeared unto them cloven tongues like as of fire, and it sat upon each of them. And they were all filled with the Holy Ghost, and began to speak with other tongues, as the Spirit gave them utterance (Acts 2:1-4).

The disciples had been patiently continuing "in prayer and supplication" (Acts 1:14), waiting for the fulfillment of the Lord's promise (Acts 1:4;8). They were obeying the Lord's clear instruction to "tarry" until they received the promise of the Father (Luke 24:49). At the appointed hour, the Holy Ghost was poured out on these faithful disciples. They were baptized with the Holy Ghost (Acts 1:5; 11:16). When they were filled with the Spirit, they "began to speak with other tongues, as the Spirit gave them

---

[95] Robertson, *Word Pictures*, 313.

utterance" (Acts 2:4). Once again, those who were baptized with the Holy Ghost immediately began to speak in tongues. This first demonstration of the Spirit's outpouring serves as the chief example of what *will* occur whenever a believer receives the gift of the Holy Ghost.

Now, let's summarize the evidence we have looked at from the book of Acts. There are five accounts in Acts (Jerusalem, Samaria, Paul, Caesarea, and Ephesus) that describe believers being baptized in or receiving the Holy Ghost. In three of these instances (2:4; 10:46; and 19:6), all who receive the gift of the Spirit spoke in tongues. Donald Johns argues that a common storytelling technique around the world is "to tell things in groups of three."[96] As he puts it, "Three times should be enough to tell anything."[97] Because speaking in tongues accompanied the baptism of the Holy Ghost in these three instances, it is rather obvious that Luke is striving to indicate that there is a close relationship between speaking in tongues and being baptized in the Spirit. Carl Brumback does not mince words, "Despite frantic efforts by some to prove otherwise, the plain and unmistakable statement of the Word is that every recipient in these instances was given utterance in tongues by the Holy Spirit."[98]

Furthermore, in the case of the Samaritans (Acts 8), it is very likely that they too spoke in tongues. To quote F. F. Bruce again, "The context leaves us in no doubt that *their reception of the Spirit was attended by external manifestations* such as had marked His descent on the earliest disciples at Pentecost."[99] Finally, while Luke does not state that Paul spoke in tongues when he was filled with the Holy Ghost, two considerations support the position that he did. First, it would be confusing and illogical for speaking in

---

[96] McGee, *Initial Evidence*, 163.

[97] Ibid.

[98] Brumback, *What Meaneth This?*, 229.

[99] Bruce, *Commentary on the Book of the Acts*, 181. Italics mine.

tongues to accompany the reception of the Holy Ghost in every other occasion in Acts except for Paul's experience of the baptism of the Holy Ghost. If the initial, physical sign is speaking with tongues, as we have argued in this chapter, then Paul had to speak in tongues, since this is the biblical evidence. Second, by Paul's own admission, he regularly spoke in tongues. As he told the Corinthians: "I thank my God, I speak with tongues more than ye all" (1 Corinthians 14:18). In the words of J. Rodman Williams, "Paul was the 'champ' in this area."[100]

Thus, the Pentecostal position that speaking in tongues is the initial evidence that a believer has received the Holy Ghost rests upon a solid biblical foundation. Indeed, as Wycoff insists, "Speaking in tongues was the normal, expected experience of all New Testament believers who were baptized in the Holy Spirit."[101] Our findings confirm the conclusion of Howard Ervin: "A baptism in the Spirit then without charismatic evidence is not a biblical datum. It is a theological construct dictated by subapostolic experience to extenuate the impotence of the Church's life and ministry in the face of secular humanism and atheistic materialism."[102] A follower of Christ who has not spoken in tongues has not been baptized in the Holy Ghost. Although he can be saved and earnest about the things of God, he is missing a glorious enduement of power from on high that will enable him to be a more effective servant of the Lord Jesus Christ.

The Incessant Evidence

There is a strange phenomenon among some groups of Pentecostals. People profess to have been baptized in the Holy Ghost because they have "spoken in tongues," despite their lives

---

[100] Williams, *Renewal Theology*, 217.

[101] Horton, *Systematic Theology*, 441.

[102] Ervin, *Spirit-Baptism*, 81

not being characterized by the holiness of Christ, a passion for souls, and a love for God's word. They have learned to go through the motions, shouting around our altars and running around our churches. Yet, when they emerge from our services, they give no indication of a changed life and a deeper walk with God. Of course, as Pentecostals, we gladly support exuberant worship and think that our churches should be marked by more demonstrative praise. However, a major problem exists when someone can "speak in tongues" and get happy during a fast song but continue to live a life that fails to display evidence of a genuine baptism in the Holy Ghost.

This issue stems from a failure to recognize that speaking in tongues is *not* the only evidence that a believer has received the Holy Ghost. The "speaking in tongues" that these hypocritical individuals engage in is, obviously, not a result of the Spirit speaking through their mouths. Maybe, it is memorized gobbledygook that they utter to seem more spiritual than they actually are. Perhaps, it is a fleshly manifestation of a carnal person. It may even be caused by a demonic influence that attempts to deceive. One thing is certain: *It is not the Holy Spirit who is behind these false utterances.* What these counterfeit tongues presuppose, though, is that there is a real, authentic baptism of the Holy Ghost evidenced by speaking with tongues available to every believer, since it would be absurd to make a forgery of an experience that did not exist.

In his classic work *Kingdom of the Cults*, Walter Martin tells the story of how the American Banking Association trains its tellers to be able to detect counterfeit money. Every year, many bank tellers are sent to Washington, D.C., in order to learn how to accomplish this important task. During their intensive training program, "no teller touches counterfeit money."[103] They handle only real, authentic money. Martin provides the justification

---

[103] Walter Martin, *The Kingdom of the Cults* (Minneapolis, MN: Bethany House Publishers, 1985), 16.

for this, "The reason for this is that the American Banking Association is convinced that if a man is thoroughly familiar with the original, he will not be deceived by the counterfeit bill, no matter how much like the original it appears."[104]

Pentecostals could learn a couple of lessons from this training strategy of the American Banking Association. First, the existence of a counterfeit confirms the existence of the original. After all, there is no such thing as a three-dollar bill, so it would be illogical to make a fake version of it. Likewise, if the outpouring of the Spirit was *not* a present availability for the people of God, then we would not expect to find the devil creating counterfeit versions. Thus, since the devil is guilty of inspiring false manifestations, we can reasonably conclude that such actions are evidence that there is a genuine moving of the Holy Ghost.

The second lesson to grasp from the American Banking Association's program is that familiarity with the original diminishes the probability of being duped by the counterfeit. Had the novice bank tellers not been utterly familiar with authentic money, they would not have been in a position to identify bogus currencies. In a similar manner, Pentecostals must be frequent participants in unadulterated Pentecostal worship to prevent the tragedy of being deceived by one of Satan's devious schemes. Once we have thoroughly familiarized ourselves with the true outpouring of the Holy Ghost, then we can evaluate other spiritual manifestations and determine whether they are of God.

Again, this aggravating problem would be less prevalent if Pentecostals would emphasize (as they already believe) that speaking in tongues is *not* the *only* evidence of Spirit-baptism. So, while we are dogmatic that anyone who has not spoken in tongues has *not* been filled with the Holy Ghost, we are equally emphatic that speaking in tongues is not the only sign that a believer has received the Holy Ghost. Pentecostal theologians, preachers, and

---

[104] Ibid.

teachers have been unanimous on this point. For instance, Carl Brumback wrote:

> The Pentecostal Movement does not teach that the glossolalia is the only evidence of the baptism with the Holy Spirit. As in apostolic days, so today there are other evidences of this experience. Our position is that He who desires to endue us with power from on high has also provided an immediate means by which we can know whether or not we have received that enduement; i.e., by speaking with other tongues as the Spirit gives utterance.[105]

Thus, since speaking in tongues is not the only evidence that a believer has received the gift of the Holy Ghost, we must search to find further biblical evidence that verify a believer's reception of the Holy Ghost. In their work *Foundations of Pentecostal Theology*, Duffield and Cleave provide a number of "permanent evidences" of the baptism of the Holy Ghost.[106] One result of being baptized in the Holy Ghost should be a greater passion for lost people. We do not mean that unbaptized believers cannot desire for souls to be saved. However, what we do mean is that this desire will be intensified as a consequence of receiving the Holy Ghost. Duffield and Cleave note, "One cannot read the history of the early Church immediately after Pentecost without realizing how there was a burning desire to proclaim the way of salvation."[107]

This is closely connected with the primary purpose of the baptism of the Holy Ghost: power for service and ministry. P. C. Nelson contended, "The Holy Spirit is not given to believers as a spiritual luxury for their personal satisfaction and enjoyment, but

---

[105] Brumback, *What Meaneth This?*, 187.

[106] Duffield and Cleave, *Foundations of Pentecostal Theology*, 327.

[107] Ibid.

as an enduement of power to fit them for bearing effective witness to the great soul-saving truths of the Gospel."[108] Howard Ervin agreed, "In the biblical context, the Christian who has been filled with the Holy Spirit is characterized by a supernatural enablement to witness for Jesus Christ."[109] In other words, a believer who receives the gift of the Holy Ghost will be empowered to fulfill the mission of God in this world.

The biblical evidence strongly confirms this perspective. Prior to his ascension, Jesus promised his apostles that they would "receive power, after that the Holy Ghost is come upon you: and ye shall be witnesses unto me both in Jerusalem, and in all Judaea, and in Samaria, and unto the uttermost part of the earth" (Acts 1:8). Earlier, he had told them that they were "witnesses of these things" and that should "tarry" in Jerusalem until they were "endued with power from on high" (Luke 24:48,49). Obviously, then, there is a close relationship between their ability to testify about what God had done for the world through Christ and their reception of Holy Ghost-power. In his comments on Luke 24, Joel Green concurred, "Luke thus draws a direct connection between their service as 'witnesses' and their reception of the Holy Spirit."[110] Therefore, any individual who claims to have received this power from on high but does not have any desire or courage to spread the gospel of Jesus Christ ought to question the validity of his experience.

Now, it must be pointed out that this purpose has been realized through the efforts of Pentecostal Christians worldwide. Since the beginning of the twentieth century, especially since the outpouring of the Spirit at Azusa Street in 1906, Pentecostals have distinguished themselves by their ardent ambition to win the world for Christ. Stanley Horton is correct in his analysis that

---

[108] Nelson, *Bible Doctrines*, 76.

[109] Ervin, *Spirit-Baptism*, 2.

[110] Joel Green, *The Gospel of Luke*. The New International Commentary on the New Testament (Grand Rapids, MI: Eerdmans, 1997), 858.

those who received the Holy Ghost at Azusa Street "were carrying the news in all directions."[111] J. Rodman Williams highlights that contemporary Christians who receive the Holy Ghost are instantly emboldened to defend God and exalt Christ. He writes:

> People who have received the gift of the Holy Spirit often demonstrate extraordinary boldness in the Lord. Particularly is this true immediately after the experience of being filled with the Spirit, when little hesitation is shown in proclaiming the word about Jesus anywhere and everywhere, and despite all opposition.[112]

Due to the courageous efforts of Pentecostal believers around the world, millions of souls have been liberated from their bondage to false gods by turning to the Lord Jesus Christ in sincere faith and repentance. God has attested the genuineness of the Christian gospel by performing extraordinary miracles. Often, these divine manifestations serve as an eye-opening introduction to the person and work of Jesus Christ. Because of their unwavering dedication to God and his word, and their firm conviction that God is a powerful God who responds to the prayers of his people, Pentecostals "have turned the world upside down" (Acts 17:6) for the sake of Christ and the glory of God. Even Larry Hart, himself not a Pentecostal, observed that "no other body of believers has lived out that Great Commission vision with greater effectiveness than the Pentecostals."[113] Time and eternity will be required to hear about the courageous exploits of Pentecostals, who, empowered by their reception of the Holy Ghost, endeavored to fulfill the Great Commission by preaching "the gospel to every creature" (Mark 16:15).

---

[111] Brand, *Perspectives on Spirit Baptism*, 52.

[112] Williams, *Renewal Theology*, 313.

[113] Brand, *Perspectives*, 96.

Another biblical evidence that the Holy Ghost has been received is that there will be "a great upsurge of joy."[114] Personal witnesses can testify that the joy that is known immediately upon receiving the Holy Ghost is indescribable, undeniable, and uncontainable. That a fullness of joy will accompany a legitimate baptism of the Holy Ghost can be demonstrated by observing the record of the early church in the book of Acts. The circumcised believers who went with Peter to Cornelius's house knew that the gift of the Holy Spirit had been poured out on the Gentiles, not only because they heard them speak with tongues, but also because they heard them *"magnify* God" (Acts 10:46). When the apostles were severely persecuted for preaching and teaching the gospel of Jesus Christ, they left the presence of their persecutors, "rejoicing that they were counted worthy to suffer shame for his name" (Acts 5:41). Although many contemporary American Christians would assume a victim mentality and cower in fear if they encountered any measure of abuse for their faith, these early believers considered this painful beating to be grounds for magnifying the One who suffered it all for them.

This unrestrained joy, in spite of any external circumstances, is present later throughout Acts. For example, the Philippian jailer "rejoiced" when he believed in God with his entire household (Acts 16:34). Furthermore, after the Ethiopian eunuch had received the instruction of Philip and was baptized in water, "he went on his way *rejoicing*" (Acts 8:39). Now, while neither of these passages explicitly mention whether these early recipients of the gospel had been baptized in the Holy Ghost, it does not seem to be a stretch to think that they also received the Holy Ghost at this time (since, in the book of Acts, water baptism is associated with receiving the gift of the Holy Ghost [2:38], even though water baptism is not necessarily required for being baptized with the Holy Ghost [Cornelius received the Holy Ghost before he

---

[114] Williams, *Renewal Theology*, 309.

was baptized in water]) and that their excessive jubilation sprang from their having been filled with the Spirit. J. Rodman Williams reasoned that, in both of these accounts, "Joy is closely connected with the Holy Spirit, quite possibly as an immediate effect of the gift of the Holy Spirit."[115] Therefore, to be filled with the Holy Ghost is to be filled with joy. It is impossible for a Spirit-filled Christian to be unjoyful.

Additional signs could be mentioned that indicate a believer has been filled with the Holy Ghost. We will end this chapter with Holdcroft's conclusion, which summarizes much of what should accompany an individual's reception of the Holy Ghost:

> Spirit baptism leads to a variety of practical results in overall Christian living. One cannot yield to receive the Spirit to indwell in His fullness without at the same time achieving a new passion for souls, a new determination to separate from the world, a new impetus for prayer, a new devotion to Scripture, and a new life of worship and praise.[116]

---

[115] Ibid., 311.
[116] Holdcroft, *The Holy Spirit*, 125.

CHAPTER 3

The Purpose of the Baptism of the Holy Ghost

The prophet Joel prophesied of a day that would come when God would pour out his Spirit on all flesh (Joel 2:28). In his great sermon on the day of Pentecost, the Apostle Peter preached that this prophecy had been fulfilled when the gathered believers "were all filled with the Holy Ghost, and began to speak with other tongues, as the Spirit gave them utterance" (Acts 2:4). This outpouring of the Spirit had been promised by Jesus himself shortly before his ascension. He told them that they would be baptized with the Holy Ghost "not many days hence" (Acts 1:5). In short, there are many purposes for which God designed this promised experience. This chapter will be dedicated to addressing a number of the purposes of being filled with the Holy Ghost. Hopefully, a greater understanding of the purposes of this post-conversion work of God will serve as a catalyst to increase your desire to experience it, so that you can more effectively carry out the Great Commission and enjoy the Spirit-filled life.

To Reveal Supernatural Manifestations

It seems reasonable to suggest that the revelation of each member of the Trinity should be accompanied by supernatural manifestations. From the very first pages of human history, God's activity has been distinguished by its supernatural nature. The Bible begins with a powerful declaration of God's existence and his creation of everything out of nothing (Genesis 1:1). Our finite minds cannot grasp the concept of nothingness. If you try to think about nothing, you will fail, because you will inevitably be thinking about something, which is not nothing. From nothing, God fashioned the galaxies, placed the stars in their silvery sockets, made the fish of the sea, and established the animal kingdom. The beginning of the universe testifies that God is a God of the supernatural.

Similarly, when the Son of God, the second person of the Trinity, took on human flesh (John 1:14) in order to "seek and to save that which was lost" (Luke 19:10), supernatural manifestations accompanied his arrival. For starters, many prophecies were fulfilled concerning virtually every aspect of Jesus' life. The birthplace of the Messiah was foretold by the prophet Micah: "But thou, Bethlehem Ephratah, though thou be little among the thousands of Judah, yet out of thee shall he come forth unto me that is to be ruler in Israel…" (Micah 5:2). Matthew records the fulfillment of this prophecy (Matthew 2:1). Furthermore, Isaiah prophesied that the coming Christ would be born of a virgin (Isaiah 7:14). That Jesus was born of a virgin is a fact provided, again, by Matthew: "When as his mother Mary was espoused to Joseph, before they came together, she was found with child of the Holy Ghost… [and she] brought forth her firstborn son: and he called his name Jesus" (Matthew 1:18,25). The perfect accuracy of these prophecies is a direct result of their divine origin.

The natural world also behaved in a supernatural fashion to signal the arrival of the promised Messiah. Matthew records the appearance of a star that informed certain wise men that the "King of the Jews" had been born (Matthew 2:2). The star supernaturally guided them to "where the young child was" (Matthew 2:9). It is no surprise, then, that the wise men "rejoiced with exceeding great joy" when they observed the star (Matthew 2:10). God had led them to the exact location of the virgin-born Savior of the world.

Moreover, the ministry of Jesus was characterized by miraculous activity. He raised Lazarus from the dead. He caused blind Bartimaeus to see. He delivered the demon possessed. He fed a multitude of people with five loaves and two fish. He calmed the raging storm. He turned water into wine. He cured lepers of their leprosy. He healed the fever of Peter's mother-in-law. Jesus was truly a divine healer who performed many miracles. What is even more impressive is that we do not know everything that Jesus did. The Gospels give us only a snippet of all his miracles. It is no exaggeration to say that Jesus' ministry was saturated with miracles. As John wrote, "And there are also *many other things which Jesus did*, the which, if they should be written every one, I suppose that even the world itself could not contain the books that should be written" (John 21:25).

Thus, when the Holy Ghost came to this world to fulfill his role in redemption, powerful manifestations also appeared with his descent. This should not appear strange to us, considering that God the Father revealed himself in divinely-inspired manifestations in the Old Testament and God the Son manifested his glory on this earth by performing many mighty deeds. Since the Holy Ghost is now the chief executor of the Trinity, we must quickly acknowledge that all his attributes, including his supernatural involvement in the affairs of humanity, will be involved in fulfilling his role in the unfolding drama of redemption.

Divine manifestations of the Holy Ghost are numerous. The gifts of the Spirit are certainly supernatural. Paul's list of these spiritual gifts establishes this point:

> For to one is given by the Spirit the word of wisdom; to another the word of knowledge by the same Spirit; to another faith by the same Spirit; to another the gifts of healing by the same Spirit; to another the working of miracles; to another prophecy; to another discerning of spirits; to another divers kinds of tongues; to another the interpretation of tongues (1 Corinthians 12:8-10).

Believers do not get to pick and choose which gifts they will be used in. Rather, it is the Spirit who controls how the gifts are used (1 Corinthians 12:11). The important part to emphasize, though, is that the Holy Ghost is interested in supernatural demonstrations of spiritual power. His will is for the church to be filled with miracles, healings, faith, words of wisdom, and prophecy. Our failure to yield ourselves fully to his authority is probably the greatest explanation for the lack of divine manifestations in our midst. If we were truly aligned with God's will, there would undoubtedly be more miraculous manifestations in our services. However, the fact that many contemporary churches witness very few (if any) demonstrations of the Spirit's power does not eliminate the truth that the Holy Ghost is, in the words of Roger Stronstad, "the charismatic Spirit of God."[117] The outpouring of the Spirit on the day of Pentecost ushered in a new era that would be characterized by prophecy, dreams, and visions (Acts 2:17-18). Thus, one of the greatest purposes of the baptism of the Holy Ghost is that it enables believers to participate in these miraculous manifestations.

To Signal Jesus' Arrival in Heaven

Another purpose of the gift of the Holy Ghost is that it demonstrated to the disciples that Jesus was at the right hand of

---

[117] Stronstad, *The Charismatic Theology of St. Luke*, 15.

the Father. Jesus informed his disciples before his betrayal that he was soon to depart: "Nevertheless I tell you the truth; It is expedient for you that I go away..." (John 16:7). Where was Jesus going? After he would suffer a brutal death by crucifixion and be raised again on the third day, he would return to the place where he came from. He explains, "I came forth from the Father, and am come into the world: again, I leave the world, and go to the Father" (John 16:28). Now, during the course of this teaching, he also revealed to his followers that they would be given another Comforter, that is, the Spirit of truth (John 14:16,17). In order for the Holy Ghost to be sent to them, it was necessary for Jesus to leave them. As he said, "If I go not away, the Comforter will not come unto you; but if I depart, I will send him unto you" (John 16:7). Not only did Jesus have to depart in order for the Comforter to be sent, but he also disclosed from where he would dispatch the Spirit: "When the Comforter is come, whom I will send unto you *from the Father...*" (John 15:26).

To put it succinctly, when Jesus withdrew from his disciples and ascended to heaven, his followers were to eagerly anticipate the arrival of the Holy Ghost. Jesus had both promised this and commanded them to "wait for the promise of the Father" (Acts 1:4). The coming of the Spirit would signify, then, that Jesus was situated at the right of the Father, prepared to perform his mediatorial work. This is exactly how Peter interpreted the events on Pentecost. In the midst of his powerful sermon, he notes how Jesus, who was exalted at the right hand of God, had poured out what "ye now see and hear" (Acts 2:33). The speaking in other tongues established the fact that this was indeed what God had proclaimed through the prophet Joel: "I will pour out of my Spirit..." (Acts 2:17). Therefore, the baptism of the Holy Ghost served the purpose of indicating to the first followers of Christ that Jesus was at the right hand of the Father.

To Empower for Mission

Arguably the greatest purpose of the baptism of the Holy Ghost is that it equips followers of Christ to fulfill God's divine mission in this world. Shortly before his ascension, Jesus told his disciples, "Behold, I send the promise of my Father upon you: but tarry ye in the city of Jerusalem, until ye be endued with power from on high" (Luke 24:49). In other words, the promise of the Father is for the distinct purpose of providing believers with miraculous strength to do mighty works for the kingdom of God and to be the powerful church that God desires. As Robert Menzies notes, ""This 'promise,' initially fulfilled at Pentecost, enables the disciples to take up their prophetic vocation in the world . . . this 'baptism in the Holy Spirit' drives them forward in the face of opposition and enables them to bear bold witness for Christ."[118]

Although we have previously devoted an entire chapter to defending what we believe constitutes the initial evidence of the reception of the Holy Ghost, it is essential to emphasize that speaking in tongues as the Spirit gives utterance is a foundational aspect to the Pentecostal worldview. We are dogmatic about this doctrine, not because we just want believers to speak in tongues, but because we maintain that tongues are a necessary sign of the glorious experience of being filled with the Holy Ghost. Any believer who has not spoken in tongues has not been a recipient of God's gracious gift of the Holy Ghost. This is why, at the beginning of the twenty-first century, we Pentecostals must announce the message, affirm the manifestations, and accept the complete fulness of the Holy Ghost's might.

A close examination of biblical truth reveals that Pentecostal power is manifested in many ways. It is impossible to write an exhaustive treatise on the workings of the Holy Ghost. However, several purposes of being baptized in the Holy Ghost will be

---

[118] Menzies, *Pentecost*, 61.

addressed to explain the meaning and necessity of this enduement of power from on high.

The first purpose to consider is that being filled with the Spirit is primarily power for service. Jesus let his disciples know that they were going to receive power when the Holy Ghost came on them, so that they would be witnesses for Christ even "unto the uttermost part of the earth" (Acts 1:8). Clearly, then, their being baptized in the Holy Ghost (Acts 1:5) is closely connected to their preaching of the gospel. P. C. Nelson agreed, writing that the baptism in the Holy Ghost results in "an enduement of power to fit them (believers) for bearing effective witness to the great soul-saving truths of the Gospel."[119] Thus, when those gathered in the upper room were filled with the Holy Ghost, they received supernatural power for the purpose of bearing record to the death and resurrection of the Lord Jesus Christ. Ray Summers observes, "This being clothed from on high was what constituted their power for witnessing. They would move out and they would speak under the controlling motivation of the power given to them by God."[120]

The justification for the preceding paragraph can be seen by examining the evangelistic fervor of the first recipients of the Pentecostal blessing. Immediately after the outpouring of the Spirit, the Apostle Peter proclaimed doctrinal and theological truths that led to three-thousand souls being saved (Acts 2:41). This zeal for evangelism continues throughout the book of Acts and is a direct result of their being filled with the Holy Ghost. Had they not been baptized with the Holy Ghost, they would not have been as enthusiastic about God's mission for the salvation of all people, and they certainly would not have been as effective.

Now, it is essential to highlight two words found in Acts

---

[119] Nelson, *Bible Doctrines*, 76.

[120] Ray Summers, *Commentary on Luke* (Waco, TX: Word Books, Publisher, 1982), 336.

1:8: power and witnesses. These two words offer tremendous insight into the effects of the enduement of power in the life of the Christian. First, power is the ability to act effectively. The power of the Holy Ghost enables the Christian to endure whatever persecution he faces when witnessing for Christ. The strengthening provided by God empowers the believer to perform mighty works that are necessary to fulfil the Great Commission. This may also be the inward strengthening of the soul or the enlightening of the mind to face persecution and persevere. The words of Apostle Paul perfectly describe the power given by the Holy Ghost: "But we have this treasure in earthen vessels, that the excellency of the power may be of God, and not of us. We are troubled on every side, yet not distressed; we are perplexed, but not in despair; persecuted, but not forsaken; cast down, but not destroyed" (2 Corinthians 4: 8-9).

Second, the word "witnesses" must not be overlooked. The Greek word for witnesses is *martus*, which renders the English word "martyr." In his great book of word studies, W. E. Vine defines *martus* as "one who can or does aver what he has seen or heard or knows... and one who bears witness by his death."[121] Throughout Acts, boldness in the face of intense persecution is a common theme. In spite of being thrown in jail or punished severely for the gospel, these early disciples continued to proclaim the message of the cross, even "rejoicing that they were counted worthy to suffer shame for his name" (Acts 5:42). The only logical explanation for such tenacity is that they were utterly convinced of Jesus' resurrection and that they were empowered by the Holy Ghost to be witnesses for Christ. Church history also records the dynamic lives of many Christian soldiers of the truth down through the centuries. These valiant warriors of the faith willingly sacrificed their lives and joined the multitudes who were martyred

---

[121] W. E. Vine, *An Expository Dictionary of New Testament Words* (New Tappan, NJ: Fleming H. Revell Company, 1966), 225.

for Christ's sake. We can gain great strength as we contemplate the ultimate price that they paid for the furtherance of the good news.

Such fearless acts of service and sacrifice require a power beyond man's ability and must come from on high. This spiritual power is provided for in the baptismal experience. To actively evangelize the world for Christ, the power of the Holy Ghost is a necessity. As Wycoff writes, "The need for supernatural power to witness and serve is the reason a distinctive experience is to be desired."[122] We shortchange ourselves when we fail to recognize that "the full dynamic of the Spirit's empowerment comes only with the special distinctive baptism in the Holy Spirit experience."[123]

The second factor that is closely connected to service is the enduement of power for spiritual warfare. The Bible teaches quite clearly that believers are engaged in an intense battle against demonic forces. Paul, for instance, reminded the saints of Ephesus that we do not wrestle "against flesh and blood, but against principalities, against powers, against the rulers of the darkness of this world, against spiritual wickedness in high places" (Ephesians 6:12). However, even though we will encounter evil powers, we have an encouraging promise: "The weapons of our warfare are not carnal, but mighty through God to the pulling down of strong holds" (2 Corinthians 10: 4). Paul's stern instruction that we "be strong in the Lord, and in the power of his might" (Ephesians 6:10) calls attention to the fulness of the baptism in the Holy Ghost in the life of the Christian. The believer who continues to be filled with the Spirit (Ephesians 5:18) is better able to fight in the spiritual warfare in the contemporary church.

It seems absurd that Christians would attempt to win the world for Christ without the provision of power available to them

---

[122] Horton, *Systematic Theology*, 451.

[123] Ibid, 448.

in the baptism of the Holy Ghost. Ray Hughes wrote, "Those who go into Christian work without this first and highest qualification find themselves at a loss to cope with the problems that arise. True love for Christ begins at the cross while power for true service begins at Pentecost."[124] In John 14:26, the Holy Ghost is called a Comforter. The Greek word for Comforter is *parakletos*, which means "called to one's side, and suggests the capability or adaptability for giving aid."[125] Thus, regardless of the battles that we will face during our daily Christian life, the overcoming, enabling power of the Holy Ghost is promised.

That the reception of the Holy Ghost is strongly commanded before endeavoring to fulfill the Great Commission can be seen by observing the sequence of events in the experience of the first disciples. Jesus commissioned them to "preach the gospel to every creature" (Mark 16:15). However, before they would be witnesses around the world, they needed to be baptized in the Holy Ghost. They were instructed to tarry in Jerusalem until they received the promise of the Father. This gift of the Holy Ghost would give them the power necessary for testifying about Christ to both Jews and Gentiles despite the efforts of wicked men to stop their progress.

We firmly believe that one of the greatest areas of spiritual warfare occurs in the arena of soul winning. Satan is not enthusiastic about evangelistic efforts. He works feverishly to ensure that unbelievers will never come to a saving knowledge of Jesus Christ. He blinds the minds of those who do not believe (2 Corinthians 4:4). In order to break the powerful stronghold of the devil over lost souls, it requires both the preaching of God's holy word and the penetrating conviction of the Holy Ghost. The Holy Ghost drives the message of Christ into the heart of

---

[124] Ray H. Hughes, *Who is the Holy Ghost?* (Cleveland, TN: Pathway Press, 1992), 71.

[125] W. E. Vine, *An Expository Dictionary of New Testament Words* (New Tappan, NJ: Fleming H. Revell Company, 1966), 298.

the hearer. As Stanley Horton asserted, "Pentecostals believe the power of the Holy Ghost is given to preach Christ... in such a way that conviction of sin takes place, lives are changed, and the Church grows."[126] This is why it is so essential for believers to be filled with the Holy Ghost. We cannot, in our own power, effectively communicate the good news. Receiving the gift of the Holy Ghost empowers ambassadors of Christ in such a way that "their preaching might be accompanied by his demonstration and power to the hearts of their hearers, so that [sinners] might believe and be saved."[127]

To be of service in the kingdom of God, and to be triumphant in spiritual warfare, requires an understanding of full dependency on the Holy Ghost. Hughes, again, stated, "Our equipment for service is neither eloquence, intellectual force, nor keenness. It is not human talent, power, or qualification. It is a power that is altogether distinct and different from all gifts of the mind, speech, and the flesh. It is the power and holy unction of God."[128] We will not succeed, and we cannot succeed, in the kingdom of God without the assistance of the Holy Ghost. The spiritual forces we fight will defeat us if we wrestle in our strength, instead of help from the Lord. Being baptized in the Holy Ghost gives us spiritual power to engage "against the rulers of the darkness of this world" (Ephesians 5:12).

The third factor to consider is that the baptism of the Holy Ghost allows a believer to be used in the manifestation of spiritual gifts. In their book *Bible Doctrines*, William Menzies and Stanley Horton write that being filled with the Holy Ghost "is the gateway into the manifold ministries of the Spirit called gifts of the Spirit,

---

[126] Brand, *Perspectives on Spirit Baptism*, 86.

[127] Adam Clarke, *Clarke's Commentary – Volume III* (Nashville, TN: Abingdon Press, n.d.), 504.

[128] Hughes, *Who is the Holy Ghost?*, 73.

including many spiritual ministries."[129] Indeed, the Pentecostal experience "leads to a life of service, where the gifts of the Spirit provide power and wisdom for the spread of the gospel and the growth of the church."[130] Having been baptized in the Holy Ghost is a prerequisite for being used in the gifts of the Spirit. Once an individual has received the gift of the Holy Ghost, he is a prime candidate for the Spirit to employ in the distribution of the spiritual gifts.

God spoke to Israel through the prophets, priests, and kings. Jesus spoke to the world through his works, his words, his virgin birth, his sinless life, his atoning death, and his justifying resurrection. Similarly, the Holy Ghost speaks to the church through many demonstrations and manifestations, including the gifts of the Holy Ghost. Words of knowledge, prophecy, tongues and interpretation—each of these supernatural gifts of the Spirit are designed to edify the body of Christ and empower the saints to fulfill God's will. Listen to the wonderful words of Lester Sumrall, "Spiritual gifts are not the icing on the cake or the meringue on the pie; they are the weapons of our warfare. The gifts of the Spirit are not designed just to make you different from other people. They are given to equip you for God's service."[131] Donald Gee provides additional insight, "They were to provide a spiritual capability far mightier than the finest natural abilities could ever supply; and, deeper still, they were to provide the supernatural basis for a supernatural order of ministry."[132]

Spiritual gifts are also divinely directed by God. It is his divine authority to distribute the gifts according to his will. He cannot be

---

[129] William W. Menzies and Stanley M. Horton, *Bible Doctrines* (Springfield, MO: Logion Press, 1999), 126.

[130] Horton, *Systematic Theology*, 450.

[131] Lester Sumrall, *The Gifts & Ministries of the Holy Spirit* (South Bend, IN: LeSea Publishing Company, n.d.), 33.

[132] Donald Gee, *Concerning Spiritual Gifts* (Springfield, MO: Gospel Publishing House, 1980), 26.

manipulated. Paul stressed that "the manifestations of the Spirit is given to every man to profit withal" (1 Corinthians 12:7). While we can avail ourselves to God by being spiritually minded and filled with the Holy Ghost, we do not earn these spiritual gifts. Some believers who have been baptized in the Holy Ghost for many decades have never been used by God in the gift of tongues and interpretation. On the other hand, other Christians who have recently received the Holy Ghost were quickly used by God in this particular spiritual gift. We must not question God's judgment but recognize that he alone is the one who chooses how the gifts will be distributed (1 Corinthians 12:11).

This is brought out clearly in the book of Hebrews. The writer illustrates this point by addressing the message of salvation and the due diligence required to faithfully obey God's word (Hebrews 2:1-4). The danger of neglect is emphatically stressed by warning that drifting from the word of truth leads to divine judgment. To completely convince the Hebrews that they had truly received the word of Christ and his apostles, God bore witness to them "with signs and wonders, and with divers miracles, and gifts of the Holy Ghost, according to his own will" (Hebrews 2:4). That God directs how spiritual gifts are employed is confirmed by the final phrase "according to his own will." It is God's will that determines how the supernatural manifestations of the Holy Ghost will operate. As Lange noted, "The distribution of the gifts and influences of the Holy Spirit in the Church is made neither accidentally nor arbitrarily, but in accordance with the will of God."[133] Horton's conclusion is worth considering:

> The Holy Spirit is sovereign in bestowing gifts.
> They are apportioned according to His will, which
> is the will of God. We can seek the best gifts, but

---

[133] John Peter Lange, *Lange's Commentary on the Holy Scriptures – Hebrews* (Grand Rapid, MI: Zondervan, n.d.), 45.

He is the only One who knows what is really the best in any particular situation. It is evident also that the gifts remain under His power.[134]

Now, importantly, each of these divine demonstrations in Hebrews 2:4 did not distract from the proclamation of the gospel but added confirmatory value to the preached word of God. Many contemporary evangelicals desire to minimize the importance of spiritual gifts, declare that they have no value, or deny their usefulness in the body of Christ. Generally, people who challenge the existence of spiritual gifts in the twenty-first century contend that the gifts of the Spirit detract from the authority of the Scriptures. However, we believe that such a position, for all its talk, is actually in direct opposition to the testimony of Scripture. As has been stated throughout this book, we believe in the Pentecostal blessing and the gifts of the Spirit, not primarily because we ourselves have experienced these marvelous manifestations of God, but because the Bible gives abundant witness that we ought to expect this Pentecostal phenomena to continue throughout the church era.

Duffield and Cleave are correct, "There is not the slightest inference in the New Testament that any endowment of the Holy Spirit would cease before seeing face to face."[135] Only theological presuppositions could cause someone to believe that spiritual gifts are not for today. Those who teach this perspective must arbitrarily assert that the baptismal experience and gifts were just for the early church and ended in the apostolic era. To justify this bankrupt doctrine, many adherents of cessationism appeal to 1 Corinthians 13:8, where Paul mentions that tongues were going to cease. Much will addressed about this verse and topic in a later chapter, but suffice it to say, Paul is *not* saying that tongues

[134] Stanley Horton, *What the Bible Says About the Holy Spirit* (Springfield, MO: Gospel Publishing House, 1976), 213.

[135] Duffield and Cleave, *Foundations of Pentecostal Theology*, 331.

(and, by implication, other spiritual gifts) will cease soon after he wrote this letter to the saints of Corinth. Many commentators understand him to be asserting that tongues will certainly cease, but not until the "perfect is come" (1 Corinthians 13:10). In other words, at the coming of the Lord Jesus Christ, the gifts of the Spirit will have fulfilled their function of edifying the church and will no longer be needed. Since the Lord has, without doubt, not returned, the task of the spiritual gifts still remains. Therefore, by virtue of simple reasoning, the gifts themselves should still exist. Words from our previous book *Tackling TULIP* are relevant to the present discussion:

> To assert that the gifts have ceased is to declare that our sovereign God is restricted in His manifestations to the church today... While intellectual elitism may be offended by emotional outbursts and manifestations of prophecy, tongues, and interpretations, the working and demonstration of the Holy Ghost will be a part of God's plan until the coming of Jesus Christ for His church.[136]

As history informs us, the gifts of the Holy Ghost did not cease with the apostles. Their continuation is confirmed by the testimony of the early church fathers, including Justin Martyr. Unfortunately, spiritual gifts have been neglected through much of church history. This does not necessarily imply that the gifts of the Spirit are unbiblical. Evangelist Zane Estes once remarked, "Just because something isn't preached doesn't mean that it isn't biblical."[137] Many glorious truths of God's word have been ignored or underappreciated by multitudes of believers since

---

[136] Grant Ralston and Edward Ralston, *Tackling Tulip* (Bloomington, IN; West Bow Press, 2019), 186.

[137] In personal conversation.

the inception of the church. Church history can certainly guide our understanding of the Bible so that we will not be deceived by any false teaching. It should not dictate our interpretation of Scripture, however. The majority is not always right, even in the Christian world. Let us not be afraid to reject popularly held beliefs when they contradict the witness of the Bible.

The baptism of the Holy Ghost and the gifts of the Spirit are available to the children of God. Howard Ervin writes, "The baptism in the Holy Spirit did not expire with Pentecost, nor even with the close of the apostolic age... It is the birthright of every Christian and represents the biblical norm for the Spirit-filled life."[138] Peter informed his audience during his sermon on the day of Pentecost that the promise of the Father "is unto you, and to your children, and to all that are afar off, even as many as the Lord our God shall call" (Acts 2:39). What seems to be undeniable is that God is calling men and women to salvation in the twenty-first century. He has not quit the task of reconciling the world to himself (2 Corinthians 5:19). We can deduce that, since he is presently calling sinners to himself, "the promise of Pentecost is still in effect."[139]

Thus, the promised baptism of the Holy Ghost is an entrance into a deeper spiritual walk with God that is accompanied by supernatural manifestations and spiritual gifts. God has designed these Pentecostal demonstrations to strengthen his people in the midst of "this present evil world" (Galatians 1:4). Furthermore, he directs how these gifts will be used during church services. His desire is for churches to frequently experience the manifestation of his presence. Any lack of the Spirit's operation in the church does not reflect God's perfect will. As Carl Brumback commented about the gift of tongues and interpretation: "It is unquestionably the will of the Lord that every local gathering of saints should

---

[138] Ervin, *Spirit–Baptism*, 26.
[139] Ibid., 27.

experience this means of edification."[140] When the gifts of the Spirit are not functioning in a local congregation, it demonstrates the lukewarmness of the people of God.

Conclusion

There are many reasons why believers should seek to be baptized with the Holy Ghost. The Pentecostal blessing provides "power for Christian service."[141] We have already demonstrated the radical transformation in the lives of the first disciples. Before the Holy Ghost was poured out on the day of Pentecost, these disciples gathered behind closed doors because they feared the Jews (John 20:19). After they received the Holy Ghost, however, "they could not be kept behind closed doors."[142] Their boldness was noticeable (Acts 4:13), and they did not cower in fear because of what might happen to them as a consequence of their courageous proclamation. They faced persecution with excitement, "rejoicing that they were counted worthy to suffer shame for his name" (Acts 5:41). Obviously, the most logical explanation behind this dramatic change in behavior is that they had been filled with the Holy Ghost. They were fighting in the Lord's army in the power of the Spirit.

This is arguably the greatest purpose for the baptism of the Holy Ghost. Contrary to the opinion of some, the same boldness that characterized the lives of the early church ought to be evident in the lives of those in the twenty-first century who receive the Holy Ghost. The Holy Ghost will empower us to perform great exploits in the name of Christ. In case you are still confused about what power the Holy Ghost provides, Duffield and Cleave describe the power that comes from on high (Luke 24:49):

---

[140] Brumback, *What Meaneth This?*, 311.
[141] Duffield and Cleave, *Foundations of Pentecostal Theology*, 312.
[142] Ibid., 313.

It is the ability to follow divine guidance into fields known only by God. It is ability to respond to divine providence. It is ability to exalt the Lord Jesus Christ. It is ability to love divinely as Jesus loved. It is ability to preach Christ with conviction and persuasion. It is ability to exercise spiritual gifts for the edification of the Church. It is ability to suffer persecution for the Lord's sake. It is ability to live a holy life above the sordid standards of the world... It is ability to work for God lovingly, willingly, faithfully, and untiringly... It is the ability to work until Jesus comes or until Earth's race is run.[143]

There is a clear purpose of the Pentecostal experience. God desires for every believer to be baptized in the Holy Ghost so that he can be a more effective tool in the kingdom of God. To be filled with the Holy Ghost is to receive power (Acts 1:8)— power to evangelize the world and win lost souls for Christ. In the wicked age that we live in, it is of utmost importance that every Christian receives the baptism of the Holy Ghost. Each of us should earnestly endeavor to obey Paul's stern command: "Be filled with the Spirit" (Ephesians 5:18).

---

[143] Ibid., 315.

CHAPTER 4

Conditions for Receiving the Baptism of the Holy Ghost

B efore addressing the conditions for receiving the baptism in the Holy Ghost, some comments concerning the baptismal experience itself need to be made. Tragically, the initial evidence of speaking in tongues as a sign of being baptized in the Holy Ghost has been misunderstood, denied, mocked, ridiculed, and scorned. Adherents of this glorious experience have been called purely emotional, hermeneutically unsound, doctrinally and theologically shallow, and woefully ignorant and unlearned. Some have went as far as to suggest that speaking in tongues is gibberish that closely resembles psychotic behavior. Nothing could be further from the truth.

What is true is that an understanding of the deeper workings of the Holy Ghost is reserved and obtained exclusively in the baptismal experience. Influential Pentecostal professor Roger Stronstad noted that "spiritual experience... gives the interpreter of relevant Biblical texts an experiential presupposition which transcends the rational or cognitive presuppositions of scientific exegesis, and furthermore, results in an understanding of empathy, and sensitivity to the text."[144] Stanley Horton signaled his support

---

[144] Qtd by Stanley Horton in Brand, *Perspectives*, 56.

of Stronstad's comment by writing that "we need both traditional Protestant hermeneutics and Pentecostal presuppositions."[145] In other words, in order to truly study the words of Scripture, it is necessary to have the same experience that the writers of the New Testament had, namely, the baptism of the Holy Ghost. This experience allows the reader to participate in the story that he is reading, rather than his just being a detached spectator, and provides him with an understanding of the Holy Ghost that cannot come from a purely scientific study of the Bible.

Throughout church history there have been many who have professed to be divine. There have also been many who have ceaselessly attacked the person and work of Christ. The apostle John addressed this issue when he wrote that "even now are there many antichrists" (I John 2:18). The book of Revelation teaches the eschatological truth of the rise of *the* antichrist in the last days. Have these antichrists or pseudo-christs succeeded in permanently impugning the holy character and reputation of Christ? We triumphantly and unequivocally declare, "Not at all!"

Many world religions claim to have their prophets and gods. However, Christianity is the only world religion that teaches the doctrine of a monotheistic, trinitarian God. Have these false religions succeeded in permanently impugning the God of Christianity? We triumphantly and unequivocally declare, "Not at all!"

First John 4:1 records, "Beloved, believe not every spirit, but try the spirits whether they are of God: because many false prophets are gone out into the world." The existence of false prophets and false manifestations throughout the church age is a known fact. John also directs us to try and prove spiritual manifestations to know if they are true or false. Have false prophets and false manifestations succeeded in permanently impugning the nature, person, and ministry of the Holy Ghost? We triumphantly and

---

[145] Ibid.

unequivocally declare, "Not at all!" The Holy Ghost, through human agency, authored the Word of God. Similarly, the Holy Ghost, through human agency, manifests Himself and speaks through His divine gifts. A true manifestation does not conflict or overshadow the inspired, inerrant word of God. It is the work of the Holy Ghost in both ministries.

When examining the Scriptures related to the promise of the baptism with the Holy Ghost, it is clear that several conditions for receiving this powerful experience are established. The enduement of power from on high is a promise, first and foremost, offered to the followers of Jesus Christ. Besides the obvious prerequisite of salvation for receiving the Holy Ghost, other conditions have been emphasized by Pentecostals, including "prayer, obedience, yielding, and expectancy."[146] In this chapter, we will address the necessary conditions for a believer to be baptized in the Holy Ghost.

① Regeneration

There are conditions that need to be met in order for someone to be saved. God is certainly the one who saves, redeems, and delivers, but he only does so once a person turns from his sins and places his faith in Christ. Similarly, before a believer can receive the deeper, fuller working of the Holy Ghost into his life, there are conditions that must be met. One thing that requires emphasis is that being baptized with the Holy Ghost enhances our love, appreciation, and gratitude for our salvation. It does not diminish the importance of being saved; rather, it builds on God's saving grace and leads to more revelations about God's redeeming power. Those who have received the gift of the Holy Ghost testify that this glorious experience has increased their affection for Jesus Christ and the work of salvation he performed in their lives.

---

[146] Horton, *Systematic Theology*, 451.

Again, the first prerequisite to receiving the promised blessing of the Holy Ghost is regeneration. This <u>first</u> step is vital to an understanding of the baptism in the Holy Ghost as a subsequent work that follows conversion. A clear demonstration of this truth appears in the story of the very first disciples. Prior to the outpouring of the Spirit on the day of Pentecost, they had already been regenerated. Jesus told his disciples that they were clean (John 13:10; 15:3). Furthermore, he informed them that even though a greater work of the Spirit was in the future, the Spirit was already operating in their lives. Listen to what Jesus said to them: "Even the Spirit of truth; whom the world cannot receive, because it seeth him not, neither knoweth him: but ye know him; for he dwelleth with you, and shall be in you" (John 14:17).

That the Spirit was working in and through the disciples before the events recorded in Acts 2 can be confirmed by observing the ministry of the seventy mentioned in Luke 10. They were given power to heal, tread on serpents and scorpions, cast out devils, and preach the message of the kingdom of God. Although Jesus cautioned them that the greater joy was that their names were written in heaven, this does not eliminate the fact that the Spirit of God had empowered them to perform these mighty deeds. These seventy disciples were "sent *(aposello)* with a commission to represent the Lord. They were therefore truly ambassadors of the King."[147] Jesus commissioned them with an important task, and he provided the required equipment to accomplish this mission.

This takes us back to John 14:17. In his commentary on the Gospel of John, Alvah Hovey adds further insight: "Whatever the Spirit may have been to the disciples, up to this moment (and we do not question his presence in their hearts), Jesus appears to have had in mind a greater manifestation of his presence and power

---

[147] Warren W. Wiersbe, *The Bible Exposition Commentary – New Testament – Vol. 1* (Colorado Springs, CO: David C. Cook, 1989), 210.

in the future."[148] Even though the disciples were regenerated and enabled by the Spirit to perform great acts for God, they still needed to be baptized with the Holy Ghost. Clearly, then, their regeneration preceded their reception of the Holy Ghost and, in fact, qualified them to be recipients of the promised blessing. Had they not been born of the Spirit, they would not have been in a position to be filled with the Holy Ghost.

The story of the great revival in Samaria (Acts 8:5-25) strengthens our position that regeneration is a necessary precondition for the baptism of the Holy Ghost. Philip preached the gospel in the city of Samaria, resulting in many coming to faith in Christ and being baptized in water. When the apostles in Jerusalem heard about the Samaritans' acceptance of the word of God, they sent Peter and John to pray for these new converts so that "they might receive the Holy Ghost" (Acts 8:15). When they arrived, they observed the testimony of the Samaritans and witnessed how they had been both saved and baptized (as a confirmation of the validity of their conversion). Consequently, Peter and John laid their hands on them, and they received the Holy Ghost.

In this passage, Luke clearly distinguishes two experiences: salvation and receiving the Holy Ghost. These men were saved, since they had received the word of God and were baptized. Had they not truly been saved, Philip would not have allowed them to participate in water baptism. Nevertheless, in spite of their salvation, they had not received the Holy Ghost. What is important to highlight is the inarguable fact that their conversion led to their being baptized in the Holy Ghost. If they had not been won to the service of Jesus the Messiah, then Peter and John would not have prayed for them to receive the Holy Ghost.

Some theologians, who find difficulty with Luke's theology,

---

[148] Alvah Hovey, *Commentary on the Gospel of John* (Valley Forge, PA: Judson Press, n.d.), 289.

strive earnestly to evade the force of Luke's record about the Samaritan revival. They generally maintain that this occurrence is an anomaly, not designed to be the norm in the history of the church. However, to us, this seems to be a common strategy for those who want the Scriptures to say what they want them to say. We agree with Luke's perspective that individuals can be believers on their way to heaven without having experienced the baptism of the Holy Ghost. We would hasten to add that believers who have not been baptized with the Holy Ghost should wholeheartedly seek this experience. It is for all believers. Those who have been saved by God's grace may enjoy this great Pentecostal gift.

One final biblical example should suffice in demonstrating the condition of regeneration for receiving the Holy Ghost. The story of the outpouring of the Holy Ghost at the house of Cornelius in Acts 10 verifies the Pentecostal perspective. Importantly, before the gift of the Holy Ghost was poured out at his house (Acts 10:45), Cornelius is described as a devout man, someone who feared God, prayed often, and gave alms. He also obeyed the word of God, had an angelic vision, and was, without question, steadfast in his daily life. These godly qualities in Cornelius caused H. A. Ironside to write, "There can be no question that he was already a regenerated man; that is born again. Of all unsaved men we read, 'There is none that seeketh after God.'"[149] His conclusion agrees with Lenski's: "All those who spoke with tongues at the time of Pentecost were already saved... All those who heard Peter in the house of Cornelius had faith and were saved before the Spirit came and gave them the ability to speak with tongues."[150]

Accordingly, a verdict can be reached after looking at the story of the early disciples, the Samaritan believers, and Cornelius. Each of these individuals had a relationship with God before

---

[149] H. A. Ironside, *Lectures on the Book of Acts* (Neptune, NJ: Loizeaux Brothers, 1972), 245.
[150] Lenski, *Acts of the Apostles*, 431.

they received the Holy Ghost. They were not depraved sinners in need of salvation; they were sincere followers of God who had been transformed by the goodness of God. J. Rodman Williams concurs with our analysis, "In all the Acts accounts of the gift of the Holy Spirit being received, there is the prior activity of the Holy Spirit in repentance and faith, or to use another term, in regeneration."[151]

Prayer

Another condition for receiving the baptism of the Holy Ghost is prayer. The significance of prayer for the reception of the Holy Ghost can be seen by examining the story of the initial outpouring of the Spirit (Acts 2). Before God poured out the Holy Ghost, approximately one hundred and twenty followers of Christ were assembled in an upper room. While waiting for the fulfillment of the promise of the Father (Acts 1:4-5), they were engaged in earnest prayer to God (Acts 1:14). Jesus had admonished the disciples during his earthly ministry to pray, and this was a lesson that they were eager to obey. They prayed fervently and unitedly in anticipation of being baptized with the Holy Ghost.

That prayer is important in this account is evident by how Luke describes the praying of the disciples: "These all continued with one accord in prayer and supplication" (Acts 1:14). Especially revealing to the serious seeker of the Holy Ghost is the significance of the word "continued" with its connection to prayer and supplication. These early disciples who had gathered in an upper room did not quickly mumble a few words to God. On the contrary, they prayed with steadfastness, with boldness, with passion, and with tenacity.[152] They would not stop praying

---

[151] Williams, *Renewal Theology*, 206.

[152] Ralph Earle, ed., *Beacon Bible Commentary – Vol. VII* (Kansas City, MO: Beacon Hill Press, 1969), 266-267.

until they had received what their souls truly longed for. As A. T. Robertson succinctly put it, "They 'stuck to' the praying... till the answer came."[153]

Additionally, toward the conclusion of Acts 4, a company of disciples "prayed," and as a result of this powerful praying, "the place was shaken where they were assembled together; and they were all filled with the Holy Ghost..." (4:31). This gathering of believers included at least a part of the five thousand converts who responded to the preaching of the Apostle Peter and John (4:4). Thus, these new believers, who had not been baptized in the Holy Ghost, were filled with the Holy Ghost in the context of this spontaneous prayer meeting. Prayer preceded and, in some sense, caused this mighty manifestation of God. Truly, God is a powerful God who responds to the prayers of his people. This is no more clearly demonstrated than with the petitions of those who yearn to receive the gift of the Holy Ghost, since, in the words of J. Rodman Williams, "In a special way it is the context or atmosphere in which the Holy Spirit is given."[154]

A further example of prayer preceding the baptism in the Holy Ghost is found in Acts 10. This entire chapter is immersed in prayer, proof that the outpouring of the Holy Ghost is dependent on people who pray. Consider, for instance, that Cornelius is identified as someone who prayed to God always (10:2) and shows prayers were "a memorial before God" (10:4). Because God accepted the prayers of Cornelius, he was visited by an angel, who confirmed that God was pleased with his prayers and gave him detailed directions about how to locate Peter (10:4-6).

Peter also was in a season of prayer when he received a revelation from God (10:9-16). The Spirit informed him that three men (from Cornelius) sought him and that he should "go with them, doubting nothing" (10:20). The Scriptures record that

---

[153] Robertson, *Word Pictures in the New Testament*, 14.

[154] Williams, *Renewal Theology*, 295.

Peter went with the messengers sent by Cornelius to Cornelius' house and preached the truth of God's word to them. While Peter was speaking, the Holy Ghost fell on the Gentiles, and they received the gift of the Holy Ghost, spake with tongues, and glorified God. Peter recognized that this activity had divine origins, as evidenced by his question: "Can any man forbid water, that these should not be baptized, which have received the Holy Ghost as well as we?" (10:47). The events in Acts 10 bring clarity to understanding the necessity of prayer for receiving the baptism of the Holy Ghost.

A final illustration that exemplifies the conditional aspect of prayer is recorded in Acts 8. After hearing that a great revival had broken out in Samaria and that many had responded to the preaching of Philip, the apostles sent Peter and John to Samaria. When Peter and John arrived, they prayed for the believers, that they might receive the Holy Ghost. Then, they laid their hands on them, and the Samaritan believers were baptized with the Holy Ghost (8:15-17). What must be emphasized is that "it was against the background and in the context of believing prayer that the Holy Spirit was received."[155]

The implication of this brief survey of prayer in Acts is simple: "If you want the empowering of the Holy Spirit, pray..."[156] In other words, there is an atmosphere conducive to receiving the gift of the Holy Ghost, and that atmosphere is marked by passionate praying. More than that, prayer creates an environment favorable for receiving and manifesting spiritual power. When we grasp this fundamental fact of the Pentecostal experience, we will view prayer not as a burden to be endured but as a glad delight to be enjoyed by committed disciples of Jesus, especially those interested in being filled with the Holy Ghost.

---

[155] Ibid., 298.

[156] John H. Hayes, ed., *Knox Preaching Guides* (Atlanta, GA; John Knox Press, 1984), 8.

Surrender

Another aspect to consider as we attempt to understand the conditions for receiving the baptism of the Holy Ghost is a personal attitude of surrender. For an individual to be saved, he must yield to God's gracious drawing. God does not coerce sinners to be saved. He extends the offer of salvation and woos them by his grace, but God will not save a sinner without the sinner's consent. Paul informed his readers that the gospel of Christ was indeed the power of God for salvation "to everyone that believeth" (Romans 1:16). An individual must yield to the convicting work of the Spirit that accompanies the preaching of the gospel in order to be saved.

This mirrors the surrender that must occur in the development of a believer who longs to receive the fullness of God's power. Complete surrender is essential to being baptized with the Holy Ghost and involves three primary elements: obedience, desire, and personal consecration. Obedience is seen immediately after the ascension, when the disciples returned to Jerusalem from Bethany and tarried in Jerusalem until they were endued with power from on high. Desire can be observed in the constant prayer and supplication for the promise of the Father to be fulfilled. Personal consecration is revealed by their worshipping Jesus at His ascension and their praising and blessing God in the temple. These three factors will be explained in more detail in the following paragraphs.

Obedience to God is discussed throughout the pages of Scripture. The record is clear that God requires, wants, and rewards obedience. This is especially true in relation to the precious gift of the Holy Ghost. Consider Peter's response to the questioning of the Sanhedrin council and high priest in Acts 5. During the course of this heated exchange, Peter proclaimed that not only is the Holy Ghost himself a witness to the death and resurrection of Christ, but he has also been given "to them that obey him" (Acts 5:32). Those who habitually disobey God and break his holy law are not candidates for the baptism of the Holy Ghost.

In addition, Paul exhorts believers to "be filled with the Spirit" (Ephesians 5:18). According to Holdcroft, "This is a passive imperative that indicates there is One to whom believers must submit."[157] The example of Paul and Ananias and their obedience to the Lord's directions in Acts 9, and the example of Peter and Cornelius and their obedience to the Lord's directions in Acts 10, serves to verify and validate God's promise to keep His word. Both acts of obedience resulted in the reception of the Holy Ghost by disciples. Because they were obedient to the guidance of God, they were soon filled with the Holy Ghost.

• The second component of a personal surrender is spiritual desire. Biblical instruction is given in many passages about sincere spiritual desire and the proper attitude for receiving the promises of God. At the beginning of the Sermon on the Mount, Jesus said, "Blessed are they which do hunger and thirst after righteousness: for they shall be filled" (Matthew 5:6). Elsewhere, it is recorded that he cried out that anyone who was thirsty could come to him and drink (John 7:37). Spiritual thirst, then, is a biblical concept. No one should expect to receive anything from God without possessing an intense thirst. This applies equally to the seeker of the baptism of the Holy Ghost. Thus, Pentecostals encourage those who need to be filled with the Holy Ghost to manifest a hunger for God and his presence. As Pentecostal theologians Duffield and Cleave add, "There must be a real hunger and thirst for more of God before one will receive the baptism with the Spirit. God does not give such gracious gifts except as they are sincerely desired and deeply appreciated."[158]

When teaching about the principles and spiritual nature of his

---

[157] Holdcroft, *The Holy Spirit*, 117.

[158] Duffield and Cleave, *Foundations of Pentecostal Theology*, 318.

kingdom, Jesus referred to the basic human properties of hunger and thirst. Every person can relate to these fundamental human desires. At some point in each of our lives, we have experienced the natural urge to eat some food or drink some water. These desires are illustrative of the intense longing man must have for the baptism of the Holy Ghost. A haphazard approach to receiving the Holy Ghost must be utterly rebuked. This indifferent attitude often expresses itself like this: If God wants me to be filled with the Holy Ghost, he will give it to me. Every believer readily understands that the blessings of the Lord must be craved before they can be received. He must seek God as a hungry, starving man craves food and a dehydrated man, dying of thirst, craves water. Hungering and thirsting after more of God results in a deeper, sanctified Christian walk and is a prerequisite to receiving the gift of the Holy Ghost.

Luke 11:9 sheds more light on the biblical teaching of spiritual desire. Here, Jesus informs his audience, "I say unto you, Ask, and it shall be given you; seek, and ye shall find; knock, and it shall be opened unto you." That praying requires persistence and intensity is revealed in this verse, indicating that the promises of God are contingent on full commitment to Christ's desires and character. Consequently, a fulfilled promise of God, such as being baptized in the Holy Ghost, enlightens the believer about what is required for God's blessings to be appropriated, encourages him to sacrifice *anything* to receive the promised gift, and empowers the believer with hope that God will favor those who seek his face. Both biblical admonitions and personal experience inform us that spiritual desire is an essential element to receiving any blessing from the Lord, including the baptism of the Holy Ghost.

So, as we consider what life consists of, and the basic needs of mankind, the Bible offers clear direction for how we can prioritize our lives. Spiritual desire must be preeminent in the life of the Christian. Jesus spelled this out: "Seek ye first the kingdom of God, and his righteousness..." (Matthew 6:33). The person who refuses to properly prioritize his life will not be a recipient of God's blessing. On the other hand, believers who respond to God's commands with immediate obedience will discover that God is truly "a rewarder of them that diligently seek him" (Hebrews 11:6).

At this point, it is necessary to correct a gross caricature of Pentecostals. Some complain that the Pentecostals' endeavor to live a sanctified life and be filled with the Holy Ghost leads to self-aggrandizement, self-promotion, and self-righteousness. To be sure, certain Pentecostals have unfortunately displayed these unholy characteristics. However, we strongly repudiate any claim that a spiritual desire to receive the baptism of the Holy Ghost results inevitably in spiritual arrogance. The "absolute and irrevocable surrender" necessary to be baptized with the Holy Ghost naturally produces a spirit of humility.[159] A spiritual thirst for God demands a humble and contrite demeanor. Anyone who exudes spiritual arrogance does not possess a genuine hunger for God's presence and power and is thus *not* filled with the Spirit.

The final aspect of surrender is personal consecration. In his book *Who Is the Holy Ghost?* Ray Hughes challenges his readers, reminding them that what the church once

> did with consecration, they now try to do with committees. What they once did with divine power, they now endeavor to do with policy. What was once done by the moving of the Spirit is now endeavored with machinery. Should the church ever forget she was born of the Holy Ghost and her life is the soul-sanctifying unction of the Holy Ghost, it will become a spiritual tomb and our church membership records will be a mere census of a cemetery.[160]

---

[159] Williams, *Renewal Theology*, 304.
[160] Hughes, *Who is the Holy Ghost?*, 73.

Some will undoubtedly criticize this emphasis on individual consecration as legalistic, self-righteous, and unnecessary. Such responses evidence a blatant disregard for what God's will is for believers. The timeless truths of God's word refute these fallacious, compromising statements. Consider Paul's remarks to the church of the Thessalonians: "This is the will of God, even your sanctification, that ye should abstain from fornication..." (1 Thessalonians 4:3). Elsewhere, he implored the church of God at Corinth: "Let us cleanse ourselves from all filthiness of the flesh and spirit, perfecting holiness in the fear of God" (2 Corinthians 7:1). He beseeched the saints in Rome to present their bodies to God as "a living sacrifice..." (Romans 12:1). He instructed them to not be "conformed to this world" (Romans 12:2). The Scriptures are abundantly clear about God's will for the Christian. While many have compromised the message of personal sanctification, God's word remains the same, and each believer must make a concentrated effort to live a holy life.

This obviously includes the believer who is seeking to be baptized in the Holy Ghost. The biblical teaching is unambiguous. Complete surrender is required to be filled with the Holy Ghost. We must submit our will to God. Duffield and Cleave highlight that "there must be a surrender of the self-will to the will of God" if one expects to be endued with power from on high.[161] Holdcroft is correct, "This 'death of self' is the gateway to the Spirit-filled life."[162] As J. Rodman Williams notes, "When self is broken of all prideful claim, a new power is released -- the power and anointing of God's Holy Spirit."[163] The passionate desire to receive the Holy Ghost results in an attitude of willingness to surrender anything and everything. This should not be mischaracterized as works of self-righteousness (as if we are earning the baptism of

---

[161] Duffield and Cleave, *Foundations of Pentecostal Theology*, 318.

[162] Holdcroft, *The Holy Spirit*, 117.

[163] Williams, *Renewed Theology*, 302.

the Holy Ghost), but it is man's responsibility to put himself in a position to receive the fullness of the Spirit of God.

③ Faith

Thus far in this chapter, we have discussed a number of conditions that must be met in order for a believer to receive the gift of the
• Holy Ghost. Individuals who have been saved by God's grace, who pray daily and diligently for this Pentecostal blessing, and who have a heart of full surrender to God are prime candidates for being baptized in the Holy Ghost. Furthermore, the conditions which have been referenced and established from the Scriptures may be better understood as expressions of faith. Ralph Riggs puts it in simple language, "They obeyed and waited; they asked by prayer and supplication (insistent asking); they believed and expressed their faith by praising and blessing God."[164] The Bible informs us that the promises of God are to be received by faith. Likewise, the baptism in the Holy Ghost is received by faith, that is – "active, obedient faith..."[165]

Obedient, active faith not only believes in the promise of God, but believes it is a personal promise. Consequently, faith motivates the believer to be engaged in persistent prayer as he yields to all conditions revealed scripturally for receiving the gift of God. It also inspires him to praise God for his faithfulness. The conditionality of the promises of God does not negate the faithfulness of God. God will fulfill his promises, including the promise of the baptism of the Holy Ghost. Faith convinces Christians that God "will give freely as we meet His conditions and ask Him for His gifts."[166] The biblical picture is of an intimate relationship between God and man. This sacred fellowship

---

[164] Riggs, *The Spirit Himself*, 108.
[165] Horton, *Systematic Theology*, 451.
[166] Riggs, *The Spirit Himself*, 106.

powerfully and perfectly reveals human responsibility cooperating with God's sovereignty to receive the fullness of God's blessings. God has established certain conditions for receiving the Holy Ghost, but once those conditions have been satisfied, he will fulfill his promise. Faith, again, characterizes the believer's pursuit of the Holy Ghost.

As we reflect on the promise and the prerequisites of being baptized in the Holy Ghost, a final word of encouragement must be offered. To every hungry and thirsty seeker of the gift of the Holy Ghost, we implore you to seek God with all your might, knowing "that waiting or tarrying before the Lord is always scriptural and is normal procedure in receiving from God."[167] The Pentecostal experience has not been changed or watered down since the initial outpouring of the Spirit, and neither has the method for receiving it. You will receive the Holy Ghost someday, so long as you do not grow weary in well doing. Wade Horton is right, "Neither the Pentecostal experience nor the Pentecostal message has ever lost the force and fire that was infused into them that first memorable day. When the same conditions are met and the same consecration is made, the same results will be seen."[168]

---

[167] Ibid., 107.

[168] Wade Horton, *Pentecost: Yesterday and Today* (Cleveland, TN: Pathway Press, 1972), 23.

CHAPTER 5

Related Issues and Questions

John Wesley is a well-known name by Christians. His sacrificial life still inspires people today. His unceasing proclamation of the gospel encourages preachers to continue to spread the good news of Jesus Christ for a lost and dying world. Although Wesley never penned a book on systematic theology, his collection of sermons and letters reveals that he had a solid grasp on biblical truth. His messages were marked by both a zeal for the lost and a love for sound doctrine. Any modern-day Christian would benefit tremendously from reading the remaining works of John Wesley.

In a sermon entitled "Satan's Devices," Wesley made an insightful comment that is relevant for the subject at hand. He lamented about "how few are able to distinguish (and too many are not willing so to do) between the accidental abuse, and the natural tendency, of a doctrine."[169] What did Wesley intend by this distinction? His point is simple. Certain doctrines held by different denominations tend to portray God in a negative light, diminish the seriousness of sin, and promote unholy living. In this case, that would be the natural tendency of the doctrine.

However, some doctrines are accidentally abused. The doctrine itself does not contradict the teachings of the Bible or

---

[169] John Wesley, *Sermons on Several Occasions* (London: The Epworth Press, 1944), 497.

encourage ungodliness, dissension, or jealousy. Nevertheless, it has been abused by advocates of it. The solution, in this instance, is not to alter the doctrine but to fix the abuse of the doctrine. The doctrine may be good and right, but susceptible to abuse. Wesley mourned the reality that few Christians have the capacity to differentiate between these two separate issues: accidental abuse and natural tendency.

While he was not discussing the baptism in the Holy Spirit,[170] Wesley's contention continues to be valid. The Pentecostal doctrine of the Spirit-baptism evidenced by speaking in tongues has certainly been abused throughout the years by many well-meaning individuals. However, I believe that these abuses are examples of "accidental abuse," not the "natural tendency" of the doctrine to lead into error. Again, the answer is to correct where the abuses have occurred (or are occurring) without eliminating this precious Pentecostal blessing. In this chapter, we will answer questions that pertain to the Pentecostal perspective on being baptized with the Holy Ghost, while also trying to address a number of accidental abuses that have occurred amongst Pentecostals.[171]

Does Every Christian Have the Holy Ghost?

At this point, it might be helpful to clarify that all Christians have the Holy Ghost, even though not all Christians have received the Pentecostal baptism of the Holy Ghost. Old-time Assemblies of

---

[170] Wesley continued his thought by discussing "the doctrine of Christian perfection."

[171] We should point out that we have already addressed many "accidental abuses" in the course of this book, including the elevation of experience over Scripture, the failure to recognize that speaking in tongues is not the only sign that a believer has been baptized in the Holy Ghost, and the mistake of not emphasizing the purpose of the baptism of the Holy Ghost. Hopefully, any remaining issues will be dealt with in this chapter.

God minister Ralph Riggs, in his book *The Spirit Himself*, noted succinctly: "All believers have the Holy Spirit."[172] It appears that there is some confusion around this issue. Many young people, raised in Pentecostal churches, have almost assumed that not every Christian has the Holy Spirit. The thinking goes something like this. Since not every believer has been baptized in the Holy Ghost, not every believer has the Holy Ghost. This reasoning is faulty, as we will explain briefly.

Consider what Paul said: "If any man have not the Spirit of Christ, he is none of his" (Romans 8:9). In other words, if a person does not have the Spirit of Christ living within him, he is not a Christian. To put it differently, no man is saved who does not have the Holy Spirit. Now, as far as I know, no trinitarian Pentecostals would argue that the baptism of the Holy Ghost is necessary for salvation. It is certainly a wonderful experience that should be sought by all Christians, but it is not required to be saved. However, if we insist (as some probably think) that those who have not been filled with the Holy Ghost do not have the Holy Ghost, then we are found to disagree with the Apostle Paul, because he declared to the Romans that any person without the Spirit of Christ does not have Christ.

The solution is to recognize that Paul is not referring to the post-conversion experience of the baptism that Luke describes in Acts. Throughout the book of Acts, receiving the Holy Ghost *is* an experience that happens after salvation. To return to a previous discussion, the Samaritan converts were saved before they received the Holy Ghost (Acts 8). Philip had preached the gospel to them, and they received the message of the cross and submitted to water baptism. Nevertheless, even though they believed in Christ, the Holy Ghost had not fallen on them yet (Acts 8:16). The apostles heard about this and sent John and Peter to them to pray for them "that they might receive the Holy Ghost" (Acts 8:15). Thus, we

---

[172] Riggs, *The Spirit Himself*, 44.

can see rather clearly that, *for Luke*, receiving the Holy Ghost is not the same experience as receiving salvation.

Unfortunately, what many Christians, influenced by popular teachers, do is to read the book of Acts in light of the writings of the Apostle Paul. They take Paul's usage of a phrase and import it into Luke's writings. This subtly gives Paul's writings more authority than Luke's writings, even though "all Scripture" has been inspired by God and is equally profitable for teaching (2 Timothy 3:16). So, two biblical authors can be using the same phrase but mean two different things. Some will no doubt protest: "It is arbitrary to assign different definitions for the same terminology." This complaint can be refuted by a cursory glance at our ordinary usage of language. There are many words that we use in multiple ways. Howard Ervin shed light on this truth:

> Words are not used univocally, that is in one sense only. In common language usage, they are used equivocally, that is with more than one meaning depending on the context. For example, the common word *ball* may mean either a spherical toy, a formal dance, or in a colloquial sense, a good time. The context is decisive for the final meaning of any word, or phrase, and not the dictionary definition.[173]

One biblical example should be sufficient for proving this contention. Paul asks the churches of Galatia a penetrating question: "Received ye the Spirit by the works of the law, or by the hearing of faith?" (Galatians 3:2). In answering the question of whether this refers to the Galatians' conversion or their reception of the baptism of the Holy Ghost, we must keep in mind that, as Ervin stated, "the context is decisive." Paul continued this portion of his letter to the Galatians by asking another question:

---

[173] Ervin, *Spirit-Baptism*, 33.

"Having begun in the Spirit, are ye now made perfect by the flesh?" (Galatians 3:3). It seems that Paul is clearly commenting about their conversion, since it is our conversion, not our reception of the Holy Ghost, that marks the beginning of our Christian life. Even most Pentecostals are willing to admit this reality.

It would be a mistake, though, to insist that what Luke writes in the book of Acts about receiving the Holy Ghost must refer to the same experience. As Ervin protested, "It is faulty methodology, however, to read Paul's usage of the phrase into the book of Acts, and to assert on that basis that Luke used the phrase with exactly the same meaning."[174] As previously mentioned, the same words can be used in various ways to convey different meanings. Both Paul and Luke should be interpreted in the context of their writings. Robert Menzies observes, "A theology of the Spirit that is truly biblical must do justice to the pneumatology of *each* biblical author."[175] So, while Paul described the Spirit's activity in primarily soteriological terms, "Luke views the gift of the Spirit *exclusively* in charismatic terms."[176] These different perspectives are not contradictory, but complementary.

Let's summarize this section by asking a question: "Does every believer have the Holy Ghost?" We feel that the biblical response to this important inquiry is yes, in a sense. The Spirit comes into our lives when we receive Christ as our personal Lord and Savior. We are set free from our bondage to sin by the "Spirit of life" (Romans 8:2). We receive new, eternal life from above. This is part of what theologians often call *regeneration*. Myer Pearlman defined this theological term like this: "Regeneration is the Divine act which imparts to the penitent believer the new and higher life in personal union with Christ."[177]

---

[174] Ibid.

[175] Menzies, Pentecost, 47. Italics his.

[176] Ibid., 48. Italics his.

[177] Myer Pearlman, *Knowing the Doctrines of the Bible* (Springfield, MO: Gospel Publishing House, 2013), 242.

However, just because all Christians have the Holy Ghost dwelling in their hearts by faith does not negate the Pentecostal contention for a post-conversion experience of spiritual empowerment. So, we must respond to the previous question that, in another sense, not every believer has the Holy Ghost. Only those who have been baptized with the Holy Ghost, according to the book of Acts, have the Holy Ghost. It is *this* experience, so powerfully presented throughout Acts, that we have argued for in this book.

Do All Speak with Tongues?

Many who object to the Pentecostal perspective on the baptism of the Holy Ghost appeal to a rhetorical question by Paul: "Do all speak with tongues?" (1 Corinthians 12:30). The way that he asks this question, along with the questions in the surrounding context, are intended to receive a negative answer. Pentecostal authors agree with this analysis. In the words of Joe Campbell, "The answer to the question is an emphatic, 'No, all do not speak with tongues.'"[178] Non-Pentecostals take this as indubitable, unquestionable, scriptural evidence that Pentecostals are in error. On the surface, this verse *does* seem to create serious trouble for anyone who believes that speaking in tongues is the initial, physical evidence that a believer has been baptized in the Holy Ghost. However, several considerations alleviate any difficulty for the Pentecostal position.

For starters, Paul himself refutes the claims of non-Pentecostals. He expresses his earnest desire that the Corinthian believers themselves speak in tongues: "I would that ye all spake with tongues" (1 Corinthians 14:5). Now, if it is absolutely certain that not every believer will speak in tongues, why would Paul state that he wants "all" the members of the church at Corinth to

---

[178] Campbell, *Warning!*, 78.

speak in tongues? Moreover, later in this chapter, he presents a situation that presupposes the entire congregation has the capacity to speak with tongues. "If therefore the whole church be come together into one place, and *all speak with tongues...*" the result would be utter confusion on the part of those who are unlearned or unbelievers (1 Corinthians 14:23). Howard Ervin rightly notes, "If *all* could not pray in tongues, contrary to the scenario here proposed by the apostle, then his argument has no relevance."[179] Thus, a brief moment of reflection is sufficient to dispel the absurdity of non-Pentecostals who cling to 1 Corinthians 12:30 as proof that Pentecostal theology is mistaken on this matter.

Another thing that must be pointed out is that those who employ this argument often *have never spoken in tongues themselves.* Joe Campbell raises this important detail and provides some noteworthy insight:

> Strangely enough this question is nearly always introduced by people who have not had the experience of speaking with tongues themselves, and who are usually bitterly opposed to speaking in tongues. When some people say that 'some do' and 'some don't,' you cannot find any of them who are the examples of the 'do's;' they are all 'don'ts'... Many people are seeking to correct and criticize what they, in their opinion, believe to be a disorder in speaking with tongues. It is strange but true that these people have never spoken in tongues themselves... yet they stand brazenly as authorities, telling what others should do, and what they should not do, with relation to speaking in tongues.[180]

---

[179] Ervin, *Spirit-Baptism*, 83.
[180] Campbell, *Warning!*, 77,87.

Furthermore, if this verse is interpreted the way that non-Pentecostals generally do, then the testimony of Acts repudiates this interpretation. *Everyone* who received the Holy Ghost in the book of Acts spoke in tongues. When the zealous disciples were filled with the Holy Ghost in Acts 2, they "began to speak with other tongues, as the Spirit gave them utterance" (Acts 2:4). When the Holy Ghost was poured out on the Gentiles, a plurality of people spoke in tongues: "They heard *them* speak with tongues..." (Acts 10:46). After Paul laid hands on the Ephesians disciples and prayed for them, they spoke with tongues (Acts 19:6). To appeal to 1 Corinthians 12:30 in arguing that tongues is not the necessary accompanying sign of Spirit-baptism does not mesh well with the accounts in Acts.

This argument by non-Pentecostals depends on a fatal misunderstanding. J. Rodman Williams explains, "Paul is dealing in the Corinthian letters with ministry in the church and how the Holy Spirit uses a diversity of gifts for building up the body."[181] Lewis Willis concurs, "A careful reading of this chapter should convince any objective reader that Paul is here referring to spiritual gifts and not to devotional tongues."[182] Thus, when Paul asks "Do all speak with tongues?" he is not asking about the sign of the baptism of the Holy Ghost; rather, "it is the gift of tongues that is being considered."[183]

A failure to differentiate between the gift of tongues and the sign of tongues has resulted in generations of believers robbing themselves of the blessed experience of being baptized in the Holy Ghost. We will not seek an experience that we think we already possess. As we seek to rightly divide the word of truth (2 Timothy 2:15), we must guard against the attempts of the enemy to defraud us of supernatural power given to believers for the express purpose of fulfilling God's mission in this world.

---

[181] Williams, *Renewal Theology*, 211.

[182] Horton, *Glossolalia Phenomenon*, 271.

[183] Ibid., 38.

The context of any passage of Scripture is crucial. It is not accidental that Paul's question is situated in 1 Corinthians 12 that is devoted to the gifts of the Spirit in the body of Christ. The Spirit distributes these spiritual gifts according to his sovereign will and purposes (1 Corinthians 12:11). Among the nine gifts listed by Paul is tongues and interpretation of tongues (1 Corinthians 12:10). Toward the end of this chapter, he makes another list, of which Paul's question about whether all speak in tongues is a part. Examining these verses is helpful in grasping the surrounding context:

> Now ye are the body of Christ, and members in particular. And God hath set some in the church, first apostles, secondarily prophets, thirdly teachers, after that miracles, then gifts of healings, helps, governments, diversities of tongues. Are all apostles? Are all prophets? Are all teachers? Are all workers of miracles? Have all the gifts of healing? Do all speak with tongues? Do all interpret? (1 Corinthians 12:27-30).

Paul establishes that God has arranged the members of the body according to the wise counsel of his will. This includes the gifts of the Spirit. Thus, when he asks "do all speak with tongues?" he is asking if all are used in the gift of tongues in the corporate assembly. Paul's next question verifies that: "Do all interpret?" The context clearly is not referring to the initial reception of the Holy Ghost, which is always signaled by speaking in tongues. So, while every believer who receives the gift of the Holy Ghost will begin to speak with tongues as the Spirit gives him utterance, not every Holy Ghost-filled saint will be used in the gift of tongues and interpretation. As Willis concludes, "Not all persons are exercised by the gift of tongues, but all persons who receive the Holy Spirit speak with evidential and devotional tongues."[184] William MacDonald agrees, "Assuredly all do not exercise the gift of tongues in the local meeting any more than that all are teachers or that all have gifts of healings."[185]

Further, MacDonald's observation is worth considering: "Not understanding the distinction between the personal and the ecclesiological *function* of glossolalia it is possible for one to become perplexed by what would doubtless seem to be contradictions in Paul's teaching and with the data…in Acts."[186] The gift of tongues and interpretation is provided by God to the church for the edification of believers. God speaks to his people through this supernatural means, and Christians who have witnessed the miraculous nature of this spiritual gift in operation should rejoice and thank God for his care, concern, and guidance. The function of the gift of tongues, however, differs from a personal, individual reception of the baptism of the Holy Ghost. We should preserve this biblical distinction, lest we settle for lukewarm, complacent Christian living without the power of the Spirit operating through us.

Did Tongues Cease?

One of the most frequent verses quoted to oppose the Pentecostal contention that speaking in tongues is for today is 1 Corinthians 13:8, which states: "Charity never faileth: but whether there be prophecies, they shall fail; *whether there be tongues, they shall cease*; whether there be knowledge, it shall vanish away." That Paul declares that tongues will cease seems to support those who insist that tongues have, in fact, ceased. Once again, a careful examination of this passage utterly repudiates this erroneous position.

---

[184] Ibid., 271-272.
[185] MacDonald, "Glossolalia in the New Testament," 67.
[186] Ibid., 63.

This viewpoint is part of a belief system known as cessationism. Basically, adherents to this theology contend that tongues, prophecies, signs, and wonders ceased during, or shortly after, the lives of the apostles. John MacArthur is probably the most well-known spokesperson for cessationism. In his sermons and through his writing, he regularly bashes Christians who believe in divine healing, prophecy, and glossolalia. To him, the practice of speaking in tongues by millions of believers worldwide is unbiblical at least and demonically inspired at worst.

In his book *Charismatic Chaos*, he uses 1 Corinthians 13:8 to argue that "tongues ceased in the apostolic age."[187] He concludes that "from the end of the apostolic era to the beginning of the twentieth century there were no genuine occurrences of the New Testament gift of tongues. They had ceased, as the Holy Spirit said they would (1 Cor. 13:8)."[188] He states that the three reasons why he is convinced of the cessation of tongues are "history, theology, and the Bible."[189] MacArthur's words and arguments deserve a response, which in turn will assist us in our understanding of why we do not think that 1 Corinthians 13:8 supports the belief that tongues have ceased.

In the matter of a few pages, MacArthur commits some serious errors. He admits, in the footnotes of his book, that "the passage does not say *when* tongues were to cease."[190] This statement is not exactly correct, since Paul suggests that the gifts of tongues, prophecy, and knowledge will continue until "that which is perfect is come" (1 Corinthians 13:10). Once this time comes, when we will be known even as we are known (1 Corinthians 13:12), "that which is in part shall be done away" (1 Corinthians 13:10). In accordance with David Garland, who is

---

[187] John MacArthur, *Charismatic Chaos* (Grand Rapids, MI: Zondervan Publishing House, 1992), 231.

[188] Ibid., 235.

[189] Ibid., 231.

[190] Ibid., 230.

representative of a plethora of biblical scholars, this "refers to the state of affairs brought about by the parousia."[191] It is "shorthand for the consummation of all things, the intended goal of creation; and its arrival will naturally displace the partial that we experience in the present age."[192]

What this indicates, then, is that[the gifts of the Spirit have been designed by God for the edification of the body of Christ for the duration of the church age] These supernatural gifts will continue to serve their purpose of strengthening the church, but "when the anticipated end arrives, they will no longer be necessary."[193] Thus, MacArthur is simply wrong that Paul does not mention "when tongues were to cease." They will cease, along with prophecy and knowledge, when the Lord returns.

MacArthur escapes the force of this passage by twisting the Scriptures to fit his own theology. After acknowledging that the "perfect" thing Paul is referring to "must be the eternal state," he argues that, in 1 Corinthians 13:8, "the language of the passage puts tongues in a category apart from prophecy and knowledge."[194] Paul used the Greek verb *katargeō* to describe the passing away of prophecies and knowledge, but he used the Greek verb *pauō* in relation to the cessation of tongues. Because of this changing in the verbs, MacArthur believes while prophecy and knowledge will be done away with when the perfect comes, "the gift of tongues will 'stop itself.'"[195] Accordingly, when tongues will cease is not mentioned by Paul, but "they won't be around when the perfect thing arrives."[196] How does MacArthur know this? He

---

[191] Garland, *1 Corinthians*, 622.

[192] Ibid., 623.

[193] Ibid.

[194] MacArthur, *Charismatic Chaos*, 231.

[195] Ibid.

[196] Ibid.

asserts, "History suggests that tongues ceased shortly after Paul wrote this epistle."[197]

MacArthur's position is false. For one thing, his insistence that Paul's change in the verbs in 1 Corinthians 13:8 is deliberate and intended to teach that tongues would cease in the first century is a blatant illustration of the weakness of his perspective. We agree with Garland's observation that the alteration of verbs is a "stylistic variation."[198] Had Paul desired to show that tongues would cease "shortly after" he wrote 1 Corinthians, he would have certainly explained this process in more detail. Further, why he would command them to not forbid speaking in tongues (1 Corinthians 14:39) when tongues were going to cease soon strikes Pentecostals as utterly contradictory.

MacArthur's claim that "tongues ceased shortly after Paul wrote this epistle" is factually incorrect. As R. Leonard Carroll asserted, "It is a mistaken assertion that the manifestation of glossolalia completely disappeared shortly after the Day of Pentecost."[199] Several witnesses could be brought to the stand to refute MacArthur's bogus contention. A brief survey of the writings of church history is sufficient to completely discredit this fallacious viewpoint. Sadly, because of his popularity, many have accepted what he has written without searching for the truth themselves. We would caution against this dangerous tendency to believe something (but especially something related to the Scriptures) *just* because of who said it. Truth is determined not by who believes what but by its correspondence to reality. If it can be demonstrated that believers spoke in tongues long after Paul wrote 1 Corinthians, this will confirm the inaccuracy of MacArthur's position and display why it is unacceptable to use 1 Corinthians 13:8 to advocate the cessation of tongues.

---

[197] Ibid.

[198] Garland, *1 Corinthians*, 622.

[199] Horton, *Glossolalia Phenomenon*, 74.

In his *Against Heresies*, Irenaeus makes a startling statement that supports our perspective that glossolalia has occurred throughout the church age. He describes "many brethren in the Church, who possess prophetic gifts" and "who through the Spirit speak all kinds of languages."[200] He continues by explaining that the purpose of these supernatural enablements is to "bring to light for the general benefit the hidden things of men."[201] It is important to emphasize that Irenaeus mentions that he is aware of "many brethren" in the church that speak, though the Spirit, in all kinds of tongues. Apparently, this was not something that only a few individuals engaged in. Further, he classifies those who possess prophetic gifts and who speak in tongues as "brethren." In other words, they were members of the family of God, not heretical fanatics. This contradicts MacArthur's argument that "the only people who claimed to have spoken in tongues" during the early centuries of the church were followers of a heretic named Montanus.[202] MacArthur ignored Irenaeus's testimony that soundly defeats his position. How convenient!

In one of his sermons, Leo the Great declared that the "sign of His Presence, *which appeared in the likeness of fire*, is still perpetuated in His work and gift."[203] Clearly, he is referring to speaking in tongues. In Acts 2:3, what appeared and sat upon each disciple was "cloven tongues *like as of fire*." Leo notes that this "sign" of God's presence has been perpetuated through the spread of the gospel. In addition to Irenaeus and Leo the Great, other ancient witnesses could be presented to corroborate our position

---

[200] Irenaeus, "Against Heresies." *The Ante-Nicene Fathers*, Vol. I, Book V., Chapter VI (Buffalo: The Christian Literature Company, 1885). Accessed with Logos Bible Software.

[201] Ibid.

[202] MacArthur, *Charismatic Chaos*, 234.

[203] Leo the Great, "Sermons of Leo the Great." *The Nicene and Post-Nicene Fathers*, Vol. XII, Sermon LXXV (New York: The Christian Literature Company, 1895). Accessed with Logos Bible Software. italics mine.

that tongues did not cease in the first century, but this endeavor would be beyond the scope of this book.

Another factor that counters MacArthur's contention is that
• millions of contemporary Christians have claimed to have spoken in tongues. According to Timothy Tennent, there are "nearly 600 million Christians around the world who are Pentecostal in belief, in practice, or by denominational affiliation."[204] Certainly, not everybody in this large body of believers has personally spoken in tongues, but they *do* believe in the practice and are often seeking to experience the promised baptism of the Holy Ghost. Again, while truth is not determined by counting noses, it is highly
• significant that "Pentecostal and charismatic Christians together make up about 27% of all Christians."[205] This multitude of tongue talkers thoroughly refutes MacArthur's perspective that tongues ceased shortly after Paul wrote 1 Corinthians.

Now, we would certainly admit that speaking in tongues did decline after the first few centuries of the church's existence. This, however, does not indicate that God was removing this miraculous gift. On the contrary, it is God's will for every believer to receive the baptism of the Holy Ghost. The reason for why speaking in tongues, prophecy, and miracles diminished was due primarily to the spiritual apathy of the church. The warning of Donald Gee is pertinent, especially for those who argue along the lines of MacArthur: "It is surely a serious thing to accuse God of *withdrawing* these gifts if the real fact is that the church *lost* them through lukewarmness."[206]

• Besides, we believe that speaking in tongues is available to believers today, not because of church history or our own glorious experiences with God, but *because of the unequivocal affirmation of*

---

[204] Timothy Tennent, *Theology in the Context of World Christianity* (Grand Rapids: Zondervan, 2007), 165.
[205] https://www.pewforum.org/2011/12/19/global-christianity-movements-and-denominations/
[206] Gee, *Spiritual Gifts*, 21. Italics his.

tongues in Scripture. MacArthur, on the other hand, subtly places a greater emphasis on history than on the Bible. However, the word of God, not church history, should be the final authority. As we argued earlier, there is no indication anywhere in the New Testament that tongues would cease sometime in the near future. Jesus specifically said that one of the signs that would accompany those that believe is that "they shall speak with new tongues" (Mark 16:17). Paul instructed the Corinthians to not eliminate tongues (1 Corinthians 14:39). No amount of exegetical gymnastics can remove the obvious implication of these verses that speaking in tongues should be practiced by believers. Tongues (along with knowledge and prophecies) will not cease until the coming of the Lord (1 Corinthians 13:8), at which point their function of building up the church will have been fulfilled.

Tongues – Evidence That Demands a Verdict

Every act of God requires evidence to confirm its existence. For example, no individual can experience the saving grace of Jesus Christ without it radically altering his life. There should be evidence in his attitude and actions that reflects the fact that he is saved. The Apostle John wrote his first epistle, in part, so that those who believe in Jesus might have assurance of their salvation (1 John 5:13). A sign that a person is a believer is if he loves the people of God. As John put it, "We know that we have passed from death unto life, because we love the brethren" (1 John 3:14). There ought to be genuine affection for other believers in the heart of every disciple of the Lord Jesus Christ.

Similarly, God has designed the experience of being baptized in the Holy Ghost in such a way that everyone who receives this precious gift might immediately know that he has received it. As we argued previously in this book, speaking with tongues is the initial evidence that a believer has been filled with the

Holy Ghost. This necessary evidence has two essential functions. First, it confirms to the recipient of the Holy Ghost that he has truly received the baptism of the Holy Ghost, not a diluted substitute. Second, it confirms to those in the company of diligent seekers of the Pentecostal blessing that a believer has actually been baptized with the Holy Ghost. The supernatural sign of speaking in tongues eliminates any ambiguity about whether someone has received the promise of the Father.

Now, why did God choose tongues to be the initial sign that a believer has been baptized in the Holy Ghost? Pentecostal writer Carl Brumback provides a few logical reasons for this decision on God's part to select speaking with tongues to be the first physical evidence of the baptism of the Holy Ghost. Perhaps the greatest explanation is that "it is a uniform evidence."[207] It does not matter whether someone is a male or a female, rich or poor, educated or ignorant, black or white. Everyone who receives the Pentecostal blessing will display the validity of their experience with the *same* sign.

One more reason should suffice to explain why God chose tongues to be the initial sign of a believer's reception of the Holy Ghost. Brumback notes how speaking with tongues "is a symbol of the Spirit's complete control of the believer."[208] This is exceedingly remarkable, given what James had to say about the tongue in his letter "to the twelve tribes which are scattered abroad" (James 1:1). He vividly describes it as "an unruly evil, full of deadly poison" (James 3:8). It "is a fire, a world of iniquity" (James 3:6). It is mysterious (even though it is an undeniable reality) how the tongue can exercise such sway over man's nature. That the tongue is the most unruly part of the body displays the wisdom of God to choose it as an illustration of the submission of one's life to the Holy Spirit. As Brumback writes, "How reasonable to expect

---

[207] Brumback, *What Meaneth This?*, 238.
[208] Ibid., 242.

BAPTIZED WITH THE HOLY GHOST

the Spirit Himself to indicate His possession of the believer by making the stubborn tongue to speak forth whatsoever He bids it."[209]

There are a number of points to consider about the practice of speaking in tongues. For starters, all manifestations of tongues are under the influence of the Holy Spirit. Although the speaker is the one who does the speaking, he is not framing the thoughts. Ray Hughes brings this out, noting that an authentic utterance in the Holy Ghost "is not a learned response. It is not a practiced response. It is not a humanly initiated action."[210] The Holy Ghost speaks through the believer as he fully yields himself to the Spirit's control. Howard Carter provides insight into this process: "Natural learning assists in no way. In speaking with other tongues the articulation is a supernatural manifestation of the indwelling Holy Spirit."[211]

A word needs to be added at this point in response to those who label the practice of speaking in tongues as incoherent babbling. Certainly, Paul never expressed that opinion. He was not adamantly opposed to tongues in the church, neither was he just a neutral bystander. He was heavily involved in speaking in tongues. Listen to his testimony: "I thank my God, I speak with tongues more than ye all" (1 Corinthians 14:18). He did not shy away from the fact that he often spoke in tongues. He thanked God that he did. To suggest, then, that speaking in tongues is nothing more than nonsensical gibberish, comparable to paganistic religions, would be to accuse the Apostle Paul of both engaging in and promoting such ungodly behavior. Surely, if the Christian version of speaking in tongues was gibberish, Paul would have not allowed it to continue. However, the tongues that

---

[210] Ray H. Hughes, ed., *The Holy Spirit in Perspective* (Cleveland, TN: Pathway Press, 1981), 39.

[211] Howard Carter, *Questions & Answers on Spiritual Gifts* (Tulsa, OK: Harrison House, Inc., 1976), 109-110.

the Holy Ghost authorizes has nothing in common with babbling or gibberish.

Another consideration is that there are different functions for speaking with tongues. When a believer is baptized in the Holy Ghost, the initial evidence is that he begins to speak in tongues as the Spirit gives him the utterance (Acts 2:4). No interpretation is required in this situation, as no interpretation was required in the book of Acts when Christians received the Holy Ghost (Acts 10:46; 19:6). Furthermore, when a Holy Ghost-filled believer prays in tongues, no interpretation is required. On this occasion, the speaker receives personal edification, as he is speaking not to men, but to God (1 Corinthians 14:2-4). However, at any time in the corporate setting, if a voice rises above all other voices as he or she speaks in tongues (even if others are also speaking in tongues), then all individuals present must yield to the operation of the gift of tongues. In this case, interpretation should follow for the edification of the body of Christ.

A final observation about tongues is how it relates to the involvement of the Holy Ghost in creation. Christianity teaches that God is transcendent. That is, he is the eternal, infinite, omnipotent Creator, the most powerful being in the universe. However, even though he reigns supreme over all that exists, he is also concerned with what he created and regularly intervenes in certain situations as he guides human history to its finality. This involvement of God within his creation has been labeled by theologians as God's *immanence*. He did not abandon that which he created. He cares about it and has chosen to be involved with it. A great illustration of his immanence is the glorious plan of redemption. God has provided a means of salvation for all men in the person and work of Jesus Christ: "For the grace of God that bringeth salvation hath appeared to all men" (Titus 2:11).

The Holy Ghost is also immanent. His immanence is expressed in various ways, from the conviction that he brings to sinners to the guidance he offers to the children of God. One of the most significant ways that the immanency of the Holy Ghost is witnessed is through the operation of spiritual gifts, as well as the speaking in tongues that accompanies being baptized in the Holy Ghost. While the Spirit is omnipresent (that is, he is everywhere at the same time), his presence can be experienced differently at different times, locations, and occasions. Allowing the Holy Ghost to operate through us for his glory and for the church's good brings about a greater sense of his nearness. As we speak in tongues, prophesy, or give words of wisdom, we are acutely aware of the Spirit's presence.

CONCLUSION

On May 22, 2019, my life (Grant) changed forever. My wife Katrina gave birth to our first child, Aiden Edward. It is impossible to adequately describe how much joy he has brought into our lives. There have certainly been challenges— from sleepless nights (mostly for Katrina) to bad diapers, from the cost of providing for a newborn baby to the stress caused by Aiden's unrelenting wailing. However, in spite of these difficulties, we would not trade Aiden for anything in the world. He is so precious to us.

In preparation for Aiden's arrival, we read a number of helpful books. We scanned the Internet in search of articles by those who had walked or were walking in our shoes. We listened to sermons and podcasts that increased our knowledge about the topic of parenting. We often thought about what it would be like to hold Aiden for the first time. We wondered what he would look like. We knew that he was a boy, but what color was his hair? Would he be a happy baby? Would he have a big head? I doubt that this behavior is abnormal for first-time parents. We were eagerly anticipating his entrance into God's beautiful world. And, it is safe to say, he has exceeded our expectations.

As I reflect on this wonderful time in my life, I have come to understand a particular truth very deeply. *Nothing could have adequately prepared me for the experience of becoming a dad.* I could have read fifty more books about what other men had written about being the father of a son, but this abundance of information could still not be a substitute for the experience of becoming a father. In other words, there is no substitute for the *experience* of being a dad.

Similarly, there is no substitute for the experience of being baptized in the Holy Ghost. We began this book by emphasizing the need to establish our doctrines according to the Scriptures. The word of God is the final authority in regard to our life, faith, and doctrine. We should believe *nothing* that contradicts the clear testimony of the Bible. With that said, this does not diminish the importance of a personal encounter with God. A man can be extremely knowledgeable about the Scriptures without being saved. Even the devil knows sound doctrine, believing that there is one God (James 2:19). The solution, of course, is not to reject the doctrines of the Bible, but to seek to personally experience them. The doctrine of salvation is profound, but spending years of diligent study about soteriology does not compare to the actual experience of salvation.

This leads us to the conclusion of the late Pentecostal Holiness preacher H. Padgett Robinson: "The folly of many would-be scholars in their treatment of Pentecost is they take the vantage point of the spectator, rather than the glorious position of the participant."[212] The baptism of the Holy Ghost is a wonderful topic to discuss and read about. However, just like with becoming a parent, there is no substitute for the experience of receiving the gift of the Holy Ghost with the evidence of speaking in tongues.

Thus, we conclude this book with a plea. Do not settle for a version of the Christian living without the dynamic baptism of the Holy Ghost. Do not be a mere spectator to the moving of the Holy Ghost. Do whatever it takes to receive the Pentecostal blessing. The first disciples were willing to tarry and pray for multiple days until they were baptized in the Holy Ghost. How long will you

---

[212] H. P. Robinson, *Heaven's Quest for a Man Like God* (Franklin Springs, GA: Advocate Press, 1969), 99.

• wait for the gift of the Holy Ghost? We pray that this book has inspired you to pursue more of God and to allow the Spirit to fully operate in your life. Friend, you can read about it, and you can study about it, but there is no substitute for the *experience* of being filled with the Holy Ghost.

BIBLIOGRAPHY

Bock, Darrell L. *Acts*. Baker Exegetical Commentary on the New Testament. Grand Rapids, MI: Baker Academic, 2007.

Brand, Chad Owen, ed. *Perspectives on Spirit Baptism*. Nashville, TN: Broadman & Holman Publishers, 2004.

Bruce, F. F. *Commentary on the Book of the Acts*. Grand Rapids, MI: Wm. B. Eerdmans Publishing Company, 1973.

Brumback, Carl. *What Meaneth This? A Pentecostal Answer to a Pentecostal Question*. Springfield, MO: Gospel Publishing House, 1947.

Campbell, Joe. *Warning! An Expose of the Devil's Counterfeit Offer Attempting to Popularize Pentecost*. Raleigh, NC: World Outlook Publications, n.d.

Carter, Howard. *Questions & Answers on Spiritual Gifts*. Tulsa, OK: Harrison House, 1976.

Clarke, Adam. *Clarke's Commentary – Volume III*. Nashville, TN: Abingdon Press, n.d.

Duffield, Guy P., and Nathaniel M. Van Cleave. *Foundations of Pentecostal Theology*. Los Angeles, CA: Foursquare Media, 2008.

Earle, Ralph, ed. *Beacon Bible Commentary – Vol. VII*. Kansas City, MO: Beacon Hill Press, 1969.

Ervin, Howard M. *Spirit-Baptism: A Biblical Investigation*. Peabody, MA: Hendrickson Publishers, 1987.

Garland, David E. *1 Corinthians*. Baker Exegetical Commentary on the New Testament. Grand Rapids, MI: BakerAcademic, 2003.

Gee, Donald. *Concerning Spiritual Gifts*. Springfield, MO: Radiant Books, 1980.

Green, Joel. *The Gospel of Luke*. The New International Commentary on the New Testament. Grand Rapids, MI: Eerdmans, 1997.

Hayes, John H., ed. *Knox Preaching Guides*. Atlanta, GA: John Knox Press, 1984.

Holdcroft, L. Thomas. *The Holy Spirit: A Pentecostal Interpretation*. Springfield, MO: Gospel Publishing House, 1979.

Horton, Stanley, ed. *Systematic Theology: A Pentecostal Perspective*. Springfield, MO: Logion Press, 1994.

--------. *Acts*. Springfield, MO: Logion Press, 2012.

--------. *What the Bible Says About the Holy Spirit*. Springfield, MO: Gospel Publishing House, 1976.

Horton, Wade, ed. *The Glossolalia Phenomenon*. Cleveland, TN: Pathway Press, 1966.

--------. *Pentecost: Yesterday and Today*. Cleveland, TN: Pathway Press, 1972.

Hovey, Alvah. *Commentary on the Gospel of John*. Valley Forge, PA: Judson Press, n.d.

Hughes, Ray, ed. *The Holy Spirit in Perspective*. Cleveland, TN: Pathway Press, 1981.

--------. *Who Is the Holy Ghost?* Cleveland, TN: Pathway Press, 1981.

Irenaeus, "Against Heresies." *The Ante-Nicene Fathers*, Vol. I, Book V., Chapter VI. Buffalo: The Christian Literature Company, 1885.

Ironside, H. A. *Lectures on the Book of Acts*. Neptune, NJ: Loizeaux Brothers, 1972.

Lange, John Peter. *Lange's Commentary on the Holy Scriptures – Hebrews*. Grand Rapid, MI: Zondervan, n.d.

Lenski, R. C. H. *Commentary on the New Testament- Acts of the Apostles*. Peabody, MA: Hendrickson Publishers, 2001.

Leo the Great, "Sermons of Leo the Great." *The Nicene and Post-Nicene Fathers*, Vol. XII, Sermon LXXV. New York: The Christian Literature Company, 1895.

MacArthur, John. *Charismatic Chaos.* Grand Rapids, MI: Zondervan Publishing House, 1992.

MacDonald, William G. "Glossolalia in the New Testament." *JETS* 7 (1964).

Marshall, I Howard. *Acts.* Tyndale New Testament Commentaries. Grand Rapids, MI: Wm. B. Eerdmans Publishing Company, 1989.

Martin, Walter. *The Kingdom of the Cults.* Minneapolis, MN: Bethany House Publishers, 1985.

McGee, Gary B., ed. *Initial Evidence: Historical and Biblical Perspectives on the Pentecostal Doctrine of Spirit Baptism.* Eugene, OR: WIPF & STOCK, 1991.

Menzies, Robert. *Pentecost: This Story Is Our Story.* Springfield, MO: Gospel Publishing House, 2013.

Menzies, William, and Stanley Horton. *Bible Doctrines.* Springfield, MO: Logion Press, 1999.

Nelson, P. C. *Bible Doctrines.* Springfield, MO: Gospel Publishing House, 1971.

Pearlman, Myer. *Knowing the Doctrines of the Bible.* Springfield, MO: Gospel Publishing House, 2013.

Ralston, Grant, and Edward Ralston. *Tackling TULIP.* Bloomington, IN; West Bow Press, 2019.

Riggs, Ralph M. *The Spirit Himself.* Springfield, MO: Gospel Publishing House, 1968.

Robertson, A. T. *Word Pictures in the New Testament — Vol. III.* New York, NY: Richard R. Smith, 1930.

Robinson, H. P., *Heaven's Quest for a Man Like God.* Franklin Springs, GA: Advocate Press, 1969.

Stamps, Donald C., ed. *The Full Life Study Bible: The New Testament.* Grand Rapids, MI: Zondervan, 1990.

Stott, John. *The Baptism and Fullness of the Holy Spirit.* Downers Grove, IL: InterVarsity, 1964.

Stronstad, Roger. *The Charismatic Theology of St. Luke.* Grand Rapids, MI: BakerAcademic, 2012.

Summers, Ray. *Commentary on Luke.* Waco, TX: Word Books, Publisher, 1982.

Sumrall, Lester. *The Gifts & Ministries of the Holy Spirit.* South Bend, IN: LeSea Publishing Company, n.d.

Tennent, Timothy. *Theology in the Context of World Christianity.* Grand Rapids, MI: Zondervan, 2007.

Torrey, R. A. *The Person and Work of the Holy Spirit.* Grand Rapids, MI: Zondervan, 1974.

Vine, W. E. *An Expository Dictionary of New Testament Words.* New Tappan, NJ: Fleming H. Revell Company, 1966.

Wesley, John. *Sermons on Several Occasions.* London: The Epworth Press, 1944.

Wiersbe, Warren W. *The Bible Exposition Commentary – New Testament – Vol. 1.* Colorado Springs, CO: David C. Cook, 1989.

Williams, J. Rodman. *Renewal Theology: Systematic Theology from a Charismatic Perspective*, Book 2. Grand Rapids, MI: Zondervan, 1996.

CPSIA information can be obtained
at www.ICGtesting.com
Printed in the USA
LVHW101033180422
716481LV00015B/84